Dedication

I am happy to dedicate this book to my devoted husband, Neigel L. Scarborough, and my beautiful daughter, Sherri LeAnn Scarborough.

To Neigel, my partner in marriage and ministry. Without his love, support, agreement, and encouragement this book would have never been published. When the battle with cancer was the fiercest, he kept reminding me of the principle: With every adversity come the seeds of fantastic future victories.

To Sherri who, though she is my daughter, is my best friend. Her fighting words during our crisis time were, "Mom, God has it all under control." I love her!

Acknowledgments

This work was originally written as a doctoral dissertation for Christian International School of Theology. Much research and personal experience went into its writing. It was as I was going through an anguishing struggle against breast cancer in 1990 that this work was birthed in my spirit. This manuscript is not, however, my work alone. I also credit the research of many men and women who are quoted throughout the book. I also credit the strengthening I received from so many people as I was going through the darkest night of the soul that I had ever experienced. I thank each one of them, and I praise God for—

The Christian International School of Theology team: John Webster, Steve Beltran, Bill Morford, and Bill Lackey who advised, read what I wrote, gave me feedback, and contributed much inspiration;

Sharon Strong, a friend who is as close as a sister and who has always been there when I needed her with her

HEALING THROUGH SPIRITUAL WARFARE

PHYSICIAN OR SUPPLIER INFORMATION

| DATE 7/16/90 | ILLNESS (FIRST SYMPTOM) OR INJURY (ACCIDENT) Infiltrative Carcinoma | HAS PATIENT HAD ILLNESS BEFORE | EMERGENCY |

PATIENT **SCARBOROUGH, Peggy E.**

DATES OF PARTIAL DISABILITY FROM THROUGH

NAME OF REFERRING PHYSICIAN **Dr. C. Scmidt**

HOSPITALIZATION DATES FROM THROUGH

ADDRESS OF FACILITY

Y ☐ N ☐ ADDRESS OF FACILITY

DIAGNOSIS

PROGNOSIS / NEGATIVE

EPSDT YES ☐ NO ☐
FP YES ☐ NO ☐

DATE OF SERVICE	FULLY DESCRIBE PROCEDURES OR SERVICES	CODE	CHARGES

SIGNATURE OF PHYSICIAN

ACCEPT GOVT CLAIMS ☐ ☐

SOCIAL SECURITY NUMBER

TOTAL CHGS   AMOUNT PAID   DUE

PHYSICIAN'S SUPPLIER'S ADDRESS PHONE NUMBER

PATIENT ACCOUNT NUMBER

Dr. Peggy Scarborough

Treasure House
An Imprint of
Destiny Image
P.O. Box 310
Shippensburg, PA 17257

"For where your treasure is
there will your heart be also." Matthew 6:21

ISBN 1-56043-796-0

For Worldwide Distribution
Printed in the U.S.A.

Treasure House books are available through these fine distributors outside the United States:

Christian Growth, Inc.
Jalan Kilang-Timor, Singapore 0315

Successful Christian Living
Capetown, Rep. of South Africa

Lifestream
Nottingham, England

Vision Resources
Ponsonby, Auckland, New Zealand

Rhema Ministries Trading
Randburg, South Africa

WA Buchanan Company
Geebung, Queensland, Australia

Salvation Book Centre
Petaling, Jaya, Malaysia

Word Alive
Niverville, Manitoba, Canada

consistent Christlike Spirit, smiling and encouraging me even as she was fighting and winning the same battle against breast cancer;

The nineteen intercessors who drove from Detroit to Ann Arbor to the hospital to war for my healing the day I went through surgery; along with ministers Floyd and Winnie Carey and Wayne Chelette;

Betty Roy, Sue Randazzo, Debbie Abbott, Donna Sommerville, Dorothy Perteet, Blanche Weldon, Mary Humphries, Nancy Smith, and many others who met early in the morning every day and prayed for my complete healing;

For the church we pastored 1986 through 1992, the Troy, Michigan, Cathedral of Praise family who were so caring;

The Women Alive intercessors from Detroit who gave me incredible strength with their encouragement, intercession, and love—for Rosemary Wilson, Madelyn Dawkins, Nicole Hendrix, Michelle Hawkins, Dorothy Twymon, Barbara Yee, and others who kept a prayer cover over me;

Herman and Doreen Smith, who counseled me to keep teaching the healing message when the vicious attack of cancer came;

Harold and Marion Spellman, who dropped all their appointments and came to me to pray until I was safe, and for the entire Peniel student body whose support I felt;

Norma Rayburn, who gave me constant support and Sharon Maloney, who prayed for me months after the crisis was over that the cancer would never return;

Norvel Hayes, whose tapes were instrumental in my healing as I played them around the clock;

Linda and Sherrill Scarborough, and Mike and Marcelle McCroskey, who encouraged me to war for my healing and then encouraged me to write this book;

Friends who were miles away from me and who prayed daily for me, including Irma Williams, Sandra Clements, Charles and Lois Beach, Euverla Hughes, Frank and Carol Catalano, Frank and Lou Tunstall;

Churches who interceded for me such as Shekinah in Ann Arbor, pastored by Paul and Barbara Yoder; and Holy Ghost Full Gospel Missionary Baptist Church, pastored by Corletta Harris Vaughan;

Our mothers, Mary Humphrey and Elzora Scarborough who showed such love;

...and the many others whom I appreciate deeply. Unfortunately time and space do not permit me to mention their contributions.

Contents

Chapter		Page

Part Three
Victories in Battle

Foreword

The truths presented in this book will bless many people. Peggy Scarborough presents these biblical principles with a balanced theological discourse and adds a powerful reality of personal conviction and life experience.

As President of Christian International School of Theology I have read numerous dissertations which have been submitted to CIST as final requirement to earn a graduate degree. Peggy has done an outstanding job of presenting the biblical truth of *Healing Through Spiritual Warfare* with a bibliography of documented confirmation which includes hundreds of scriptures verifying this truth.

As an active prophet of God within the Church for the last 40 years and author of three books on the prophetic, I can assure you that Peggy's presentation in her chapter on "warring with the weapon of the prophetic word" is biblically sound and true to the life experience of thousands of believers. Anyone ready with an open mind and a believing heart will be blessed, healed and spiritually equipped to become an effective and mature soldier in the army of our Lord Jesus Christ.

Dr. Bill Hamon
Bishop/President/Founder Christian International

Author: *The Eternal Church;*
              Prophets and Personal Prophecy;
              Prophets and the Prophetic Movement;
              Prophets, Pitfalls and Principles ; and
              Fulfilling Your Personal Prophecy.

Peggy Scarborough has spent hour upon hour researching and putting together material that will help people who are in need of some kind of miracle in their life, particularly a healing miracle. Hosea says that people perish for lack of knowledge and the author of this book is instructing people as to how to receive from the Lord Jesus Christ.

Having been healed of metastatic cancer of the liver, after being given only a few weeks to live in 1981, I can attest to the healing power of the Lord Jesus Christ. I owe my life to Him and am so grateful to be alive. Like Peggy, John and I are interested in helping people. We salute her for her efforts in helping multitudes of people.

Dodie Osteen
Wife of John Osteen
Lakewood Church, Houston, TX

Healing Through Spiritual Warfare is an inspiring account of one of my dearest friend's struggles for victory over breast cancer, a testimony of the tremendous healing she received, and a shining witness to the glory of God surrounding her life.

Christians must learn to do battle against sickness and disease. Peggy Scarborough declares, "God has a battle plan." From her own experiences as a warrior on the front lines of the combat zone, she has written this practical, scripturally-based manual to instruct the believer on how to wage war for his own healing by employing weapons of spiritual warfare.

This book is a powerful weapon—a tool in the hands of God to bring healing to those who will believe that "getting healed through warfare is worth the fight."

Healing Through Spiritual Warfare is a ringing call to battle for all who earnestly desire victory in their war for healing, and a challenge to any child of God who needs an answer to the question, "How can I be healed?"

Dr. Marion Spellman
Peniel Ministries
Johnstown, Pennsylvania

It always refreshes my heart to hear a new voice articulate with such Spirit-filled anointing and scriptural authority the divine provision that God has made for us regarding physical healing. An integral part of the Pentecostal heritage has been a strong theological position that in the atonement, God has provided healing for all. In a day when liberal Protestantism would deny the demonstration of God's miracle-working power; in a day when satan would seek to steal the birthright from the children of God; it is imperative that the church reaffirm her doctrinal stance concerning divine healing and again proclaim that it is both God's nature and promise to heal the sicknesses of His people. This is exactly what Peggy Scarborough does in this magnificent book. I appreciate the biblical thoroughness in which she treats her subject and the simplicity of language in which she clothes her thoughts and communicates her burden. I have great respect for the personal dedication of this great lady and the dexterity and skill that is exhibited through her writing. I highly recommend this book for your prayerful consideration and contemplation.

Dr. T.L. Lowery
Pastor, National Church of God
Washington, DC

Introduction: The Problem, the Attack, and the Solution

Nothing is more devastating than hearing the words, "You have cancer." It is also a frightening experience to suddenly discover that you have sugar diabetes or some other life-threatening disease. When times such as these come, most people in the body of Christ do not know what to do. When given such a diagnosis, many people listen to the doctor's statistics and give up, often dying prematurely. When this happens to a family member or close friend, the reaction is usually to begin preparing for the loved one's eventual death. This book has been prepared to provide an alternative response in such cases. Drawing from much research and personal experience, the author offers a biblically-based prescription that will work.

You Don't Have to Die Prematurely

The truth is, you don't have to die prematurely. The psalmist said, "I shall not die, but live, and declare the works of the Lord" (Ps. 118:17). This book deals with what a person can do so that he may live and not die. It will also examine what we can do to get our loved ones healed.

Spiritual Warfare is the Answer to Sickness

The central theme of this book concerns warring in order to get well. However, the writer found many during her research who did not like the idea of getting involved in spiritual warfare. They felt that they had come to Christ as a lamb, but now were being told they had to go to war. But whether we like it or not, the devil has already declared war on us. It is now up to us to learn how to fight.

God Himself is a warrior. The Bible says, "The Lord is a man of war: the Lord is His name" (Ex. 15:3). God therefore has a battle plan for His people. We can count on Him to teach us how to war if we are willing to learn.

An awakening about spiritual warfare is taking place in the earth today. God is raising up warriors to go into cities and nations to pray against prevailing principalities and powers. After days of intense prayer, many major strongholds have been broken. It is believed by many that the communist stronghold fell in Russia because of the intercessors who had been flying to Russia and standing in Red Square, pulling down the strongman over Russia through intercession. I personally took a large group of intercessors into downtown Detroit, into the very heart of the city, to pray for the city. The devil, however, launched a counterattack. I went through a vicious battle with breast cancer. Through this experience, I learned to war and won. It is God's will that we learn to war against sickness, just as we must against sin.

We Must Locate the Enemy

We must understand that our war is against satan. Men and women in the Air Force are given a book called *Doctrines of War*.[1] The introductory chapter states that the first principle of warfare is to know your enemy. As Christians begin to understand that overcoming sickness involves warfare, they will be better equipped to fight. Sickness comes from the devil. Jesus said, "The thief cometh not, but for to steal, and to kill, and to destroy: I [Jesus] am come that they might have life, and that they might have it more abundantly" (Jn. 10:10). Jesus told Peter, "Satan hath desired to have you" (Lk. 22:31). This shows us who our enemy is.

When a person gets sick, satan taunts by saying, "There is no hope. No one ever gets healed from your disease, especially in the stage where you are. I've got you. I've got you. You're going to die." This is warfare!

Satan is the Enemy of God

Satan hates humanity because he hates God and everything that is like God. When he attacks with sickness and disease, his finest weapons, his goal is to harm what God has made in His likeness. Every time satan hurts a Christian, he hurts the heart of God, because God loves His children so much.

Satan is the Enemy of Christians

Satan hates the bodies of those who are called to carry out the purposes of God. Every time he sees a human being looking and acting like God, his hatred is kindled afresh against humanity. Every time he sees a Christian, he is reminded of God, the object of his wrath. If he can attack the Christian's body, he can stop or hinder the work of God on the earth, for without a healthy body a Christian cannot live in the fulness God desires. If satan can attack a dedicated Christian's body, he can stop the attack against his kingdom. He can hinder or even stop the Christian from fulfilling the ministry God has called him to do. Sometimes his attacks are counterattacks in retribution for some defeat he has experienced because of the warrior's ministry.

Sickness is Part of the Enemy's Warfare

Peter Wagner says, "Approximately 25 percent of Jesus' healings as recorded in the gospel of Mark involve demons."[2] The devil also uses the natural results of the fall of man to cause sickness. He uses bacteria, viruses, malnutrition, accidents, fights, poison, rapists, murderers, etc. Regardless of the cause, the outcome of sickness is pain, suffering, and even death, which are all the works of satan.

Demons Whose Business is to Make People Sick

Satan has many demons whose chief business is to make people sick. When dealing with sickness, one must be aware of these various evil spirits. For instance, Benny Hinn maintains that three demonic spirits come along with cancer: the spirit of infirmity, the spirit of fear, and the spirit of bondage.[3] Anyone who is attacked by cancer will have to battle and defeat these spirits. Many other sicknesses are caused by spirits and must be dealt with similarly.

God Does Not Will Sickness

Sickness and disease do not come from God. This belief alone is one of the devil's chief tricks to deceive the Church. If it were God's will for a Christian to be sick, then he should not go to the doctor. But the Bible declares that God is the Lord who heals you. He heals all who come to Him. God's plan is for Christians to be well.

Learning to War for Healing

The primary purpose of this book is to teach God's people how to war for healing. When attacked by the devil, a person does not have to die. Instead, he should declare war on the sickness. Though we may not like war, we must understand that even the Kingdom of God suffers violence. Jesus reminded us in Matthew 11:12 that from the time John the Baptist began preaching the Kingdom, the Kingdom suffered violence, and the violent took the Kingdom by force. From out of nowhere violence comes to assault God's people. There is a war going on and we are involved in it. Ephesians 6 tells us that "we wrestle not against flesh and blood, but against principalities, against powers... ." We wrestle against the rulers of the darkness of this world.

But our war is different. The warriors are not necessarily dressed in combat boots. Sometimes they are dressed in pretty dresses and high-heel shoes. Sometimes they are not physically strong. Sometimes they are young; sometimes they are old. But God's warriors can become mighty warriors.

We do not have the same weapons that the world has, yet the weapons of our warfare are mighty through God. We wage war in a different way. We wage war by prayer. We wage war by confession. We wage war by resistance. We wage war by singing. We wage war by forgiving our enemies. We wage war by practicing gentleness. We wage war by giving up hatred and bitterness. We wage war with the truth. We wage war by feeding the hungry. We wage war by speaking in tongues. We wage war by fasting. We wage war by surrendering our wills to God. We wage war by healing the sick and in many other ways that we will explore in this book.

Furthermore, we have a host of angels, a heavenly Air Force that fights for us. We are the ground troops. We confront the enemy on earth in the physical realm, while our angelic cohorts confront them from above in the spiritual realm. We do not fight alone. We fight where we are. Sometimes we fight in the marketplace. Sometimes we fight the enemy in our homes. Sometimes we do battle with him in the hospital. But our fight is fixed. Jesus has already won the battle. We just have to enforce it.

This book will discuss various methods that God will use to bring about healing. His goal is that the healed person would take the gospel of healing to the world. Chapter 1 will deal with knowing what God thinks about healing. The reader will see God's will in the Old Testament, the New Testament, in the early Christian Church, and in the Church today.

Chapter 2 will explore areas in the warrior's personal life that will bring healing. It will reveal areas in the sick person's life that will bring great spiritual strength. Subjects such as getting well as a priority, having the will to live, developing a fighting spirit, knowing your authority, a change in mentality, visualization, goal-setting, healing words, and dealing with fear will be discussed. Biblical nutrition will also be examined and the part it plays in the healing process. The associations the person desiring to be healed has will also be explored. The kind of conversation that brings about an atmosphere of healing will be discussed, along with the role of fasting, speaking in tongues, and laughter. In addition, the subject of watching what the Father is doing in healing will be examined.

Chapter 3 will emphasize healing through three powerful weapons: the Word of God, the name of Jesus, and the blood of Jesus. These are the warheads that will bring destruction to the devil and release the power of healing in our bodies.

Chapter 4 will examine God's battle plan for healing. The missiles that take the powerful warheads to their target will be thoroughly explored. God dwells in the praises of His people, and I know of numerous people who have been healed during a time of worship. Praise and worship will therefore be reviewed first. The other missiles that launch the warheads are prayer, confession, resistance, binding and loosing, preaching, testimony, breaking generational curses, and many more. This chapter will show how these missiles move the warheads to the point of attack and bring about healing.

Chapter 5 will reveal how a person can be healed through warfare prophecy. This is another of the weapons, which due to its uniqueness, has an entire chapter dedicated to it. When one of God's prophets speaks concerning the healing of an individual, the sick person can war with that prophecy. This chapter will examine how a person can prophesy concerning his own healing. We can hear the voice of God for ourselves. Areas will be explored such as how a bad prophecy can be reversed, and why some people die when it has been prophesied that they will live.

In Chapter 6, I share with you my personal battle with cancer, as well as other instances of healing. Chapter 7 is a review of the battle plan.

There are Adversaries to the Healing Message

There are many who feel strongly that healing should not be emphasized today. Peter Wagner, in his book *How to Have a Healing Ministry in Your Church*, tells of one scholar who was quoted anonymously in *Christianity Today* as criticizing John Wimber and Peter Wagner for teaching a course about signs and wonders at Fuller Theological Seminary. He criticized them for teaching a lottery-type Christianity in which there must be a few big winners—spectacular healings—and many $10 winners—cured headaches—in order to attract a crowd. His major objection was that such teaching is far from a proper theology of the cross.[4]

There are great difficulties that exist and many objections that may be raised against a theory of healing which differs from the accepted methods. There are those who argue that a study on warring for healing is not necessary. Satan, especially, will not like this study. The recommended way to deal with the enemy is to resist him. The Bible never says that the best way to handle the devil is to ignore him.

Also, there will be those who feel that the recomendations of this book are too difficult for a sick person to actually put into practice. The *Air Force Promotion Fitness Examination Study Guide* states: "The study of war is complicated because war is complicated."[5] This is not a study for those looking for an easy road. Engaging in warfare is an arduous business, but the victory is well worth the fight.

The time is ripe to wipe out the deep pessimism which most Christians and ministers have about disease.

When a Christian is told that he has an incurable disease, this does not automatically mean he has to die. Christians do not have to accept as inevitable the many aggravating diseases that the devil puts upon them. This is the purpose of this book. I pray that it will be a tool in the hands of God to bring healing to many people.

Warfare Healing Principles

- God Himself is a warrior.

- You must locate the enemy.

- The devil has declared war on you.

- Sickness is part of the enemy's warfare in the earth.

- Sickness and disease do not come from God.

- With cancer come three spirits: spirit of infirmity, spirit of fear, and spirit of bondage.

- There are special evil spirits whose assignment is to make people sick.

- You must declare war on sickness and disease.

Endnotes

1. U.S. Air Force, *Doctrines of War* (Washington D.C.: U.S. Air Force, 1992), p. 4.

2. Peter Wagner, *How to Have a Healing Ministry in Any Church* (Ventura, CA: Regal Press, 1988), p. 109.

3. Benny Hinn, *Divine Healing*, Tape 3, Orlando Christian Center, n.d.

4. Wagner, p. 109.

5. Department of the Air Force, *Training Promotion Fitness Examination Study Guide* (Washington D.C.: U.S. Air Force, 1992), p. 15.

Part One

The Warrior's Preparation for Battle

Chapter One

Knowing What God Thinks About Healing

God has a will concerning healing. The most important thing in spiritual warfare is knowing what God's will is. It makes little difference what other people say about healing. The question that must be asked is, "What did God say about it?" Before anyone can war for healing for himself or for another person, he must be rid of all uncertainty concerning God's will in the matter.

Warring faith cannot go beyond one's knowledge of what the revealed will of God is. One must know what the Scriptures plainly teach, that it is just as much God's will to heal the body as it is to heal the soul. Until we know what God's will is, there is nothing to base our warring or our faith on.

Praying for healing with the faith destroying words, "If it be thy will" is not warring. It is destroying the sick person. The prayer that will bring healing follows knowing the word upon which alone faith is based. "Himself bare our sicknesses" (Mt. 8:17) is just as much a part of the gospel as His words, "Who his own self bare our sins in His own body on the tree" (1 Pet. 2:24).

Healing and Salvation Go Hand in Hand

Healing and salvation go hand in hand throughout scripture. To say healed or to say saved means the same thing. The word saved in Romans 10:9 is the same Greek word used by Mark when he said, "as many as touched Him were made whole." Both words saved and made whole were translated from the Greek word, sozo. T.L. Osborn tells us that each of the words found in the following scriptures are translated from the same Greek word sozo: healed—Mark 5:23; saved—Mark 16:16; healed—Luke 8:36; saved—Acts 2:21; healed—Acts 14:9; saved—Ephesians 2:8; saved—Luke 18:42; saved—James 5:15; made whole—Mark 5:34; be whole—Mark 5:28; whole—Luke 17:19; whole—Acts 4:9; saved—Acts 4:12; made whole—Mark 6:56.[1]

Healing is Heaven's deposit for the glorified body which we will receive in the future. The devil's desire is to see you sick or dead, but Jesus came to bring us life…and that more abundantly.

What the Godhead Says About Sickness

God called sickness "captivity." "The Lord turned the captivity of Job when he prayed for his friends" (Job 2:10). Jesus called sickness "bondage": "Ought not this woman, whom Satan has bound, be loosed from this bond" (Lk. 13:16). The Holy Spirit calls sickness "oppression": Acts 10:38 says, "Jesus went about doing good and healing all that were oppressed of the devil."

There are many scriptures in the Old Testament that show the attitude of God the Father toward sickness. The New Testament reveals the attitude and works of Jesus in bringing healing. We further see the numerous miracles and healings through the early church. Today that same power continues through those who dare to be obedient to God's Word. We will now examine some of the many Scriptures concerning healing.

What God Says in the Old Testament About Healing

God said...

1. I am the Lord that healeth thee (Ex. 15:26).
2. Your days shall be one hundred and twenty years (Gen. 6:3).
3. Thou shalt be buried in a good old age (Gen. 15:15).
4. Thou shalt come to thy grave in a full age like as a shock of corn cometh in his season (Job 5:26).
5. When I see the blood, I will pass over you and the plague shall not be upon you to destroy you (Ex. 12:13).
6. I will take sickness away from the midst of you...and the number of your days I will fulfill (Ex. 23:25-26).

7. I will not put any of the evil diseases of Egypt upon you; but I will lay them upon all them that hate you (Deut. 7:15).

8. If you keep my commandments...I will prolong your days...that your days may be multiplied, and the days of your children...as the days of heaven upon the earth (Deut. 11:8-9,21).

9. I turned the curse into a blessing unto you, because I love you (Deut. 23:5 and Neh. 13:2).

10. I have redeemed you from every sickness and every plague (Deut. 28:61 and Gal. 3:13).

11. As your days, so shall your strength be (Deut. 33:25).

12. Not a word failed of any good thing which the Lord had spoken...All came to pass (Josh. 21:45).

13. I have heard thy prayers, I have seen thy tears: behold, I will heal thee (2 Kings 20:5).

14. I have found a ransom for you, your flesh shall be fresher than a child's and you shall return to the days of your youth (Job 33:24-25).

15. I have healed you and brought up your soul from the grave; I have kept you alive from going down into the pit (Ps. 31:1-2).

16. I will give you strength and bless you with peace (Ps. 29:11).

17. I will preserve you and keep you alive (Ps. 41:2).

18. I will strengthen you upon the bed of languishing; I will turn all your bed in your sickness (Ps. 41:3).

19. I am the health of your countenance and your God (Ps. 43).
20. No plague shall come near your dwelling (Ps. 91:10).
21. I will satisfy you with long life (Ps. 91:6).
22. With long life I will satisfy you, and show you my salvation (Ps. 91:16).
23. I forgive all thine iniquities and heal all your diseases (Ps. 103:3).
24. I sent my word and healed you and delivered you from your destructions (Ps. 107:20).
25. You shall not die, but live, and declare the works of the Lord (Ps. 118:17).
26. I heal your broken heart and bind up your wounds (Ps. 147:3).
27. The years of your life shall be many (Prov. 4:10).
28. Trusting me brings health to your navel and marrow to your bones (Prov. 3:8).
29. My words are life to you and health (medicine) to all your flesh (Prov. 3:8; 4:22).
30. My good report makes your bones fat (Prov. 15:30).
31. Pleasant words are sweet to your soul and health to your bones (Prov. 16:24).
32. My joy is your strength. A merry heart doeth good like a medicine (Neh. 8:10; Prov. 17:22).
33. The eyes of the blind shall be opened. The eyes of them that see shall not be dim (Is. 32:3; 35:5).

34. The ears of the deaf shall be unstopped. The ears of them that hear shall hearken (Is. 32:3; 35:5).
35. The lame man shall leap as a deer (Is. 35:6).
36. The tongue of the dumb shall sing (Is. 35:6).
37. You restored me to health and let me live (Is. 38:16).
38. I give power to the faint and strength to them that have no might (Is. 40:29).
39. I will renew your strength. I will strengthen and help you (Is. 40:31; 41:10).
40. To your old age and gray hairs I will carry you and I will deliver you (Is. 46:4).
41. I bore your sickness (Is. 53:4).
42. I carried your pains (Is. 53:4).
43. I was put to sickness for you (Is. 53:10).
44. With my stripes you are healed (Is. 53:5).
45. I have seen your ways and will heal you (Is. 57:18).
46. I will heal you (Is. 57:19).
47. Your light shall break forth as the morning and your health shall spring forth speedily (Is. 58:8).
48. I will restore health unto you, and I will heal you of your wounds (Jer. 30:17).
49. Behold, I will bring health and cure, and I will cure you and will reveal unto you the abundance of peace and truth (Jer. 33:6).
50. I will bind up that which was broken and will strengthen that which was sick (Ezek. 34:16).
51. Behold, I will cause breath to enter into you and you shall live, and I shall put My Spirit in you and you shall live (Ezek. 37:5).

52. Withersoever the rivers shall come shall live. They shall be healed and everything shall live where the river comes (Ezek. 47:9).
53. When I passed by thee and saw thee polluted in thine own blood, I said unto thee when thou wast in thy blood, live; yea I said unto thee when thou wast in thy blood, live (Ezek. 16:6).
54. Seek me and you shall live (Amos 5:4,6).
55. But unto you that fear My name shall I arise with healing in My wings (Mal. 4:2).
56. Come and return unto Me; I will heal you and I will bind you up (Hos. 6:1).
57. When you are weak, say I am strong (Joel 3:10).

Types of Healing in the Old Testament

The Passover Lamb

When the children of Israel were slaves in Egyptian bondage and remembered that they were children of promise, they cried out to God and He sent them a deliverer. Through Moses, God sent ten horrible plagues upon Egypt, which finally persuaded Pharaoh to let God's people go. Before the tenth plague struck, Moses told the people to kill a lamb for every household and sprinkle its blood on their doorposts. They were then to roast and eat the lamb. The death angel passed through Egypt that night killing all the firstborn of both man and beast. But wherever the angel saw the blood sprinkled on the doorposts of an Israelite home, he passed over and spared their firstborn. That night, their faith in the blood of the lamb healed everybody who was sick and strengthened all who were weak. According to the Bible, three million people were completely well at one time. These Israelites were slaves and had certainly been ill-fed and ill-treated. But God sent them the miracle of the slain lamb. What a beautiful picture of Jesus Christ, the Lamb of God, who heals and delivers us.

The Brazen Serpent

After the Israelites left Egypt, they failed to realize how great God had been to them and got themselves into much trouble with God. Their continual complaining finally brought God's judgment upon them. Poisonous serpents began to bite them and many were dying. Moses prayed for the people, and the Lord instructed him to make a serpent of brass. He was then to put it on a pole and lift it up where all who had been bitten could see it. As many as beheld it would be healed and would live. Jesus referred to this incident when He said, "And as Moses lifted up the serpent in the wilderness, even so must the Son of man be lifted up: that whosoever believeth in Him should not perish, but have eternal life" (Jn. 3:14-15). Both healing and forgiveness came through this type of the atonement. Thus healing and salvation both still come as we behold Jesus Christ, the crucified One. Both are still provided for us today.

The Cleansing of the Leper

Leviticus 14 and 15 contains the ordinances whereby the priests were to make atonement for the cleansing of the lepers. The types in these chapters show that it was invariably through atonement that sickness was healed. All of these typical atonements pointed to and prefigured Calvary. If the type brought healing, how much more will the real Christ heal?

The priest was to take two living clean birds, cedar wood, scarlet, and hyssop. He was to kill one of the birds in an earthen vessel over fresh, running water. He then was to take the living bird, the cedar wood, the scarlet material, and the hyssop, and dip them in the blood of the dead bird. The blood was then to be sprinkled on the leper seven times. Afterward, the priest was to pronounce the leper clean and let the living bird go into the open heavens.

The bird had been taken down from the open heavens and taken captive. This represents God's holy Dove, who of His own choosing came down from the realm of glory to man. He made Himself a captive dove. God gave Him a human body. He was not captive in a cage, but was captive because He was in a body of flesh, to be sacrificed for mankind. The bird that was slain had no choice, but God's Dove laid His life down of His own choosing to bring healing to man.

The bird had to be clean. Jesus was the clean, pure, perfect sacrifice. This was God's Dove, clothed in the holiness of God. Jesus took our sicknesses into His own body. Jesus did away with all the products of sin through His own body.

The cedarwood symbolizes the cross to which Jesus was bound. The scarlet thread represents the cord that tied Jesus to the cross. The running water represents the living Word of Jesus. He washes and cleanses us by His Word.

When the leper saw that blood-soaked bird fly away, he knew that he was home free. His leprosy was over.

The dead bird represents the death of Christ. The living bird represents the resurrection of Christ. The healed leper is symbolic of the one needing to be healed. It can happen because of the death and resurrection of Jesus Christ. The leper got healed based on the shadow or type. May God give us the revelation that we can be healed based on a better hope—the real sacrifice of Jesus Christ.

What Jesus Says in the
New Testament About Healing

1. I will, be thou clean (Mt. 8:3).
2. I took your infirmities (Mt. 8:17).
3. I bore your sicknesses (Mt. 8:17).
4. If you are sick, you need a physician. I am the Lord your physician (Mt. 9:12).
5. I will come and heal him (Mt. 8:7).
6. I am moved with compassion toward the sick and I heal them (Mt. 14:14).
7. I heal all manner of sickness and all manner of disease (Mt. 4:23).

8. According to your faith, be it unto you (Mt. 9:29).

9. I went about all the cities and villages, teaching in their synagogues and preaching the gospel of the Kingdom and healing every sickness and every disease among the people (Mt. 9:35).

10. I give you power and authority over all unclean spirits to cast them out, and to heal all manner of sickness and all manner of disease (Mt. 10:1; Lk. 9:1).

11. I healed them all (Mt. 12:15).

12. If at any time you should see with your eyes and hear with your ears, and understand with your heart, and be converted, I will heal thee (Mt. 13:15).

13. As many as touch Me are made perfectly whole (Mt. 14:36).

14. Healing is My children's bread (Mt. 15:26).

15. I do all things well. I make the deaf to hear and the dumb to speak (Mk. 7:37).

16. Every plant which My heavenly Father hath not planted shall be rooted up (Mt. 15:13).

17. If two of you agree on earth concerning anything that they ask, it will be done for them by My Father in Heaven (Mt. 18:19).

18. If you can believe, all things are possible to him that believeth (Mk. 9:23; 11:23-24).

19. When hands are laid on you, you shall recover (Mk. 16:18).

20. My anointing heals the brokenhearted, and delivers the captives, recovers sight to the blind, and sets at liberty those that are bruised (Lk. 4:18; Is. 10:27; 61:1).
21. I heal all those who have need of healing (Lk. 9:11).
22. My servants go forth through the towns, preaching the gospel and healing every where (Lk. 9:6).
23. I am not come to destroy men's lives but to save them (Lk. 9:67).
24. Behold, I give you authority over all the enemy's power and nothing shall be any means hurt you (Lk. 10:19).
25. Ought not this woman, being a daughter of Abraham, whom satan hath bound, be loosed from this bond (Lk. 13:16).
26. My power is present to heal (Lk. 5:17).
27. I sent them to preach the Kingdom of God and to heal the sick (Lk. 9:2).
28. Heal the sick and say unto them, the kingdom of God is come nigh unto you (Lk. 10:9).
29. In Me is life (Jn. 1:4).
30. I am the bread of life. I give you life (Jn. 6:33,35).
31. The words I speak unto you are Spirit and life (Jn. 6:63).
32. I am come that you might have life, and that you might have it more abundantly (Jn. 10:10).
33. I am the resurrection and the life (Jn. 11:25).

34. If you ask anything in My name, I will do it (Jn. 14:14).
35. Faith in My name makes you strong and gives you perfect soundness (Acts 3:16).
36. I stretch forth My hand to heal (Acts 4:30).
37. I, Jesus Christ, make you whole (Acts 9:34).
38. I do good and heal all that are oppressed of the devil (Acts 10:38).
39. God wrought special miracles by the hand of Paul; so that from his body were brought unto the sick handkerchiefs or aprons, and the diseases departed from them (Acts 19:12).
40. The law of the Spirit of life in Me has made you free from the law of sin and death (Rom. 8:2).
41. The same Spirit that raised Me from the dead now lives in you and that Spirit will quicken your mortal body (Rom. 8:11).
42. Your bodies are my members (1 Cor. 6:15).
43. Your body is the temple of the Holy Ghost, and you are to glorify Me in your body (1 Cor. 6:19-20).
44. If you will rightly discern My body which was broken for you, and judge yourself, you will not be judged and you will not be weak, sickly, or die prematurely (1 Cor. 11:29-31).
45. I have set gifts of healing in My body (1 Cor. 12:9).
46. My life shall be made manifest in your mortal flesh (2 Cor. 4:10-11).

47. I have delivered you from death; I do deliver you; and if you trust me I will yet deliver you (2 Cor. 1:10).

48. I have given you My name and have put all things under your feet (Eph. 1:21-22).

49. I want it to be well with you and I want you to live long on the earth (Eph. 6:3).

50. I have delivered you from the authority of darkness (Col. 1:13).

51. I will deliver you from every evil work (2 Tim. 4:18).

52. I tasted death for you. I destroyed the devil who had the power of death. I have delivered you from the fear of death and bondage (Heb. 2:9,14-15).

53. I wash your body with pure water (Heb. 10:22; Eph. 5:26).

54. Lift up the weak hands and the feeble knees. Don't let that which is lame be turned aside but rather let Me heal it (Heb. 12:12-13).

55. I, Jesus Christ, am the same yesterday, today, and forever (Heb. 13:8).

56. Let the elders anoint you and pray for you in My name, and I will raise you up (Jas. 5:14-15).

57. Pray for one another and I will heal you (Jas. 5:16).

58. By My stripes you were healed (1 Pet. 2:24).

59. My divine power has given unto you all things that pertain to life and godliness through the knowledge of Me (2 Pet. 1:3).

60. Whosoever will, let him come and take of the water of life freely (Rev. 22:17).
61. Beloved, I wish above all things that you may prosper and be in health even as your soul prospers (3 John 2).

For a picture of the healing ministry of Jesus, carefully read the following accounts:

The healing of the man with the unclean spirit: Mk. 1:23; Lk. 4:33.

The healing of Peter's mother-in-law: Mt. 8:14; Mk. 1:30; Lk. 4:38.

The healing of multitudes: Mt. 8:16; Mk. 1:32; Lk. 4:40; Mt. 12:15; Mk. 3:10; Mt. 14:34; Mk. 6:55; Mt. 4:23; Lk. 6:17; Mt. 9:35; Mt. 11:4; Lk. 7:21; Mt. 14:14; Lk. 9:11; Jn. 6:2; Mt. 15:30; Mt. 19:2.

The healing of the leper: Mt. 8:2; Mk. 1:40; Lk. 5:12.

The healing of the man with palsy: Mt. 9:2; Mk. 2:3; Lk. 5:17.

The healing of the man with the withered hand: Mt. 12:9; Mk. 3:1; Lk. 6:6.

The healing of the demoniac of Gadara: Mt. 8:28; Mk. 5:1; Lk. 8:26.

The healing of Jairus' daughter: Mt. 9:18; Mk. 5:22; Lk. 8:41.

The healing of the woman with the issue of blood: Mt. 9:20; Mk. 5:25; Lk. 8:43.

The healing of a few sick people: Mt. 13:58; Mk. 6:5.

The healing of the Syrophoenician's daughter: Mt. 15:22; Mk. 7:24.

The healing of the deaf and dumb man: Mk. 7:32.

The healing of the blind man: Mk. 8:22.

The healing of the child with an evil spirit: Mt. 17:14; Mk. 9:14; Lk. 9:38.

The healing of blind Bartimaeus: Mt. 20:30; Mk. 10:46; Lk. 18:35.

The healing of the centurian's servant: Mt. 8:5; Lk. 7:2.

The healing of two blind men: Mt. 9:27.

The healing of the dumb demoniac: Mt. 9:32.

The healing of the blind and dumb demoniac: Mt. 12:22; Lk. 11:14.

The healing of the blind and lame man in the temple: Mt. 21:14.

The healing of the widow's son: Lk. 7:11.

The healing of Mary Magdalene and others: Lk. 8:2.

The healing of the woman bound by satan: Lk. 13:10.

The healing of the man with dropsy: Lk. 14:1.

The healing of the ten lepers: Lk. 17:11.

The healing of Malchus' ear: Lk. 22:49.

The healing of the nobleman's son: Jn. 4:46.

The healing of the impotent man: Jn. 5:2.

The healing of the man born blind: Jn. 9:1.

The healing of Lazarus: Jn. 11:1.

Christ used the same word to rebuke sickness and evil spirits. In his book *Bodily Healing and the Atonement* Dr. T.J. McCrossan writes, "Christ always uses the same harsh Greek word, *epitimao*, to rebuke sickness as He used to rebuke evil spirits. In Luke 4:35 we read, 'And Jesus rebuked (*epetimésen*) him (the evil spirit) saying hold thy peace and come out of him.' In Luke 4:39 we read, 'and he stood over Simon's wife's mother, and rebuked (*epetimésen*), the same word as in Luke 4:35 the [spirit of] fever; and it left her.' Christ used the same harsh word to rebuke all sicknesses as he used to rebuke all evil spirits, because all sickness is caused by Satan."[2]

Healing in the Atonement

When Christ died, He died for our sicknesses as well as for our sins. McCrossan quotes Young, Leeser, and McLaren: "The same two verbs 'borne' (*nasa*) and 'carried' (*sabal*) of Isaiah 53:4—where we are told, 'Christ bore our sicknesses and carried our pains')—are the very same two verbs used in Isaiah 53:11-12 to express the great truth that Christ bore vicariously our sins and our iniquities."[3] This shows us through scholarly evidence that healing is definitely in the atonement.[4]

What the Early Church Thought About Healing

After Jesus ascended, He continued His healing ministry through His disciples. McCrossan re-translates Peter's explanation of the healing of the man who was born blind: "Peter says of this wonderful cure (Acts 3:16): 'If we this day be examined of the good deed done to this sick man, by what means he has been cured (*sesostai*, saved); Be it known unto you all...that by the name of Jesus Christ of Nazareth, whom ye crucified...even by him (*touto*, by this one) does this man stand here before you whole.' By here using *touto*, the dative case of the demonstrative pronoun *houtos* (the dative of instrument), Peter declares to us that this miracle was performed directly by the Lord, by the Spirit, just as all the miracles recorded in Matthew 8:16."[5]

McCrossan reminds us that Christ performed all the miracles after Pentecost by the Spirit. He says, "They prayed in Acts 4:28,30: '...Grant unto thy servants, that with all boldness they may speak thy word, by thyself stretching forth the hand of thyself for physical healing (*eis iasin*).' This is an exact literal translation, and clearly proves that Jesus Christ, the Lord, by the Spirit, continued to heal the sick after Pentecost."[6]

What God Is Saying Today About Healing

God is no respecter of persons (Acts 10:34), and He never changes (Mal. 3:6). What He said in the Old and New Testaments He is saying today. Since the very same Holy Spirit who raised Christ from the dead and who did all the miracles of the disciples dwells in us today, we can expect this same Jesus to continue His miraculous work by this same Spirit.

Furthermore, many miracles have been witnessed in recent years which show that God is still healing today. Examples of modern-day healings will be reviewed throughout this book.

Dr. McCrossan shows us the work of the Holy Spirit in manifesting the life of God (*zoe*) in our physical bodies. He translates Romans 8:11 this way: "But if the Spirit of Him that raised up Jesus from the dead dwell in you, He that raised up Christ from the dead shall also quicken (*zoópoiései*) your mortal bodies by His Spirit that dwelleth in you."[7] McCrossan points out, "This verb 'will quicken' is *zoópoiései* and comes from *zóé* (life) and *poieó* (I make)."[8] It is the work of the Holy Spirit to keep making life in these mortal bodies of ours.

We have seen in this chapter what God thinks about healing. We have seen how Jesus went about healing all who were sick and oppressed of the devil. We have also seen how He continued His healing ministry through the early Church and is still carrying out His work today through His body in the earth.

In the chapters that follow, we will examine His warriors and His weapons. God has a battle plan, and He will help us in the battle. Romans 8:26 reads, "Likewise the Spirit also helpeth our infirmities: for we know not what we should pray for as we ought; but the Spirit itself maketh intercession for us with groanings which cannot be uttered." According to Dr. McCrossan, the word translated "helpeth" means "take hold, together with, against."[9] Picture the Holy Spirit taking hold together with you against the power of the enemy. We do not war alone. He wars with us.

Warfare Healing Principles

- The most important thing in spiritual warfare is knowing what God's will is.

- Praying for healing with the faith destroying words, "If it be thy will" is not warring. It is destroying the sick person.

- Healing and salvation go hand in hand throughout Scripture.

- God called sickness captivity.

- Jesus called sickness bondage.

- The Holy Spirit called sickness oppression.

- When Christ died, He died for our sicknesses as well as for our sins.

- Healing is in the atonement.

- Jesus continues His healing ministry through His body in the earth.

Endnotes

1. T.L. Osborn, *Healing the Sick* (Tulsa, OK: Harrison House, Inc., 1951), pp. 36-37.

2. T.J. McCrossan, *Bodily Healing and the Atonement* (Tulsa, OK: Kenneth Hagin Ministries, 1982), p. 2.

3. Ibid, p. 22.

4. Ibid, p. 2.

5. Ibid, p. 19.

6. Ibid, p. 20.

7. Ibid, p. 38.

8. Ibid.

9. Ibid, p. 13.

Chapter Two

The Warrior's Life Style

When a person suddenly learns that he has a serious illness, he will inevitably have to war through depression, denial, anger, and hurt. This can be draining to the physical body, as well as to the spirit and the soul. The purpose of this chapter is to show how to war in getting well and living to declare the works of God.

The Priority Is Getting Well

A person wanting to be healed must make getting well his top priority. Once he has chosen to live, his life style may then need to be drastically altered. To make the needed changes will often involve a real spiritual fight. For example, he may find ordinary conversation to be utterly meaningless. When table talk becomes empty, irrelevant conversation, the warrior may need to leave and get alone with God in prayer. He may need to encourage himself in the Word. This is not a time for mere talking; it is a time to war. With such a war going on, the person who has decided to fight for his life may appear at times to be out of touch. But the impending victory is worth the battle.

The Will to Live

The starting point is the will to live. Dodie Osteen, who was diagnosed as having liver cancer, often says that you have to be feisty to get healed. Dr. Bernie Siegel refers to an article about cancer in a 1985 issue of *Lancet*, a British medical journal. He reports, "This study of fifty-seven women diagnosed with early breast cancer ten years before revealed that after the first five years, reoccurrence-free survival was significantly commoner among patients who reacted to cancer by a fighting spirit than among patients who responded with stoic acceptance or feelings of helplessness...After ten years, their survival statistics showed that 70 percent of the fighting spirit patients were still alive versus 50 percent of the deniers."[1] This principle of having a "fighting spirit" is a critical component of the sick person's life style. For anyone to help the person get well or to pray the prayer of faith for him, the person himself must have an intense desire to live.

State Aloud One's Plan to Get Well

It is important for the sick person to state aloud his plan to live and get well. When Terry Law was given the prognosis that his sugar diabetes was incurable, he told the doctors, "I will get well."[2] He later explained that he felt it was important for him to establish immediately his intention to live. Today he is a healed man with a great ministry.

The sick person needs to hear himself say that he is going to get well. Other people need to hear him say it. The devil also needs to hear the words, "I will get well."

Knowing One's Authority

Jesus gave His followers authority. Anyone who intends to war for his healing must know his authority and must surround himself with people who know their authority. They must see that in Christ they are a possesser of Christ's authority. We are what He is. We are in Him. Christ lives in us.

Too many Christians do not believe enough concerning their spiritual authority. The devil has deceived them into thinking they are nobodies, with no power to stop him from anything he is doing. In his book *The Saints at War*, Frank Hammond states, "Before we enter the arena of conquest against the devil...we must know who we are in Christ and know the spiritual power and authority invested in us by Christ."[3] The reason we have authority over the devil is because we are already seated with Christ in His throne.

This will be one of the most difficult battles for the sick person to win. When a doctor gives him a bad report, it can be devastating to his faith. Then, when he reads the statistics of the survival rate, that is enough to throw him completely into depression. When he is then told that he must understand that he has authority over his sickness, it may be difficult for him to exercise his authority, the enemy having made him believe that he is not in control of his life. This is especially the case when the disease is cancer or some other life-threatening disease. But he absolutely must thoroughly understand his authority if he is to have confidence in getting well.

Change in Mentality

Many sincere Christians become overwhelmed with shame and condemnation when they get sick. This is because they feel that God must be displeased with them or they have sinned. Joyce Boisseau in *You Can Live in Divine Health* argues,"Realistically, sickness is on the earth. It affects the righteous, the holy, the innocent, the young, the old, the mother, the father, the president, the pope, the kings and princes, the rich and the poor, the high and the lowly, the beast, the fowl, and the fish, the soil, the air and the water. The earth is cursed with sickness…And all of us who are of the earth are subjected to that curse, regardless of our spirituality."[4] In order to war effectively, one must grasp that it is not a shame to be sick. When Job's comforters come with the question, "What have you done to cause this?" the best answer is, "I am simply under attack from the enemy."

The sick person must understand where the battle is coming from and why. Possibly the enemy sees in the person the seed of some unique ministry, and he is trying to kill it before it is birthed.

The sick person must not get it into his mind that God is chastening him. A Scripture that is often used to justify sickness as chastening is this: "Whom the Lord loveth He chasteneth" (Heb. 12:6). T.L. Osborn argues, "This Scripture does not say: 'whom the Lord loves He makes sick, or smites with disease.' It does not say 'God imparts disease to or makes infirm every child whom he receives.' "[5] He continues, "The word 'chasten' comes from a Greek word which means 'instruct, train, discipline, teach or educate' like a teacher instructs a pupil or like a parent teaches and trains a child. When a teacher instructs, various means of discipline and training may be employed in the education process, but never sickness."[6] He further maintains, "Satan will constantly condemn you by bringing to your mind every mistake you have ever made, offering his lying suggestion: That is why you are sick…Your God is chastening you…and there is no hope for you…Your adversary, the devil, therefore succeeds in causing you to blame God, the Healer of sickness, for the very sickness Satan has put upon you."[7] God has the Word and the Holy Spirit to instruct His children, not cancer or arthritis or some other disease.

Knowing That God Has No Favorites; He Heals All

The sick person must understand that everyone can be healed. Jesus healed all who came to Him. T.L. Osborn in *Healing the Sick* says, "Until you are fully convinced that God wants you to be well, there will always be a doubt in your mind as to whether or not you will be healed. As long as there is that doubt in your mind, perfect faith cannot exist; and until faith is exercised, without doubt or wavering, you may never be healed."[8] Until it becomes clear to the sick person that it is God's will to heal "all," he will always wonder if he is one of the unlucky ones that God may not be wanting to heal.

It is easy to believe that God can heal, but when a person is sick, it is also easy to wonder if God will actually heal him. E.W. Kenyon said, "It was a great comfort to my heart when I realized that the Father has no favorites...Everyone has the same rights in the family."[9] Kenyon further argues that, "Because God laid your sickness on Jesus and made Him sick with your diseases, Satan has no right to put on you what God put on Jesus."[10] He translates Romans 6:14: "For sin shall not Lord it over you."[11]

When God brought the children of Israel out of their bondage in Egypt, He held a gigantic healing crusade. He announced Himself to be the healer of His people with these words: "I am the Lord that healeth thee" (Ex. 15:26). He spoke these words to all three million people who had been in Egypt. The Bible says that when God brought them forth, there was not one feeble person among their tribes (Ps. 105:37). God is bound by His covenant to continue healing all who are sick and weak. He must do this to fulfill His words: "My covenant will

I not break, nor alter the thing that is gone out of My lips" (Ps. 89:34). If God had changed His mind concerning healing, He would have told us.

It is not necessary to try to explain away why some people are not healed. In her book *Balm of Gilead*, Lillian Yeoman writes, "How much precious time I wasted trying to explain Mrs. So and So's case. But one day I got desperate and said, 'I don't care if every saint on earth dies of this disease, the Word of God promises me healing and I take it, and I have it.' "[12] She went on to say, "I have had it ever since."[13] This must become the attitude of everyone who wars for healing.

Seeing Oneself Well

It is essential that the sick person see himself as being well, since people usually live out their mental images whether it be sickness or health. Charles Capps recalled an article entitled "Patient Knows Best," which appeared in the August 1991 issue of *Reader's Digest*:[14]

A person's answer to the question, "Is your health excellent, good, fair or poor?" is a remarkable predictor of who will live or die over the next four years according to new findings.

A study of more than 2800 men and women 65 and older found that those who rate their health poor are four to five times more likely to die in the next four years than those who rate their health excellent. This was the case even if examinations show the respondents to be in comparable health.

These findings are supported by a review of five other large studies, totaling 23,000 people, which reached similar conclusions, according to Ellen Idler, a sociologist at Rutgers University, and epidemiologist Stanislav Kasl of Yale University School of Medicine, co-authors of the new study.

People whose image of themselves is one of being in poor health will talk about their poor health, whether imagined or actual. Even though they may begin in good health, they will eventually live out the image they have of themselves, even unto death.

Calling Things That Be Not as Though They Were

There is probably no subject as important to healing and health as the principle of calling things that are not as though they were. God called Abram the father of nations before Sarah ever gave birth to the promised child, and He taught Abram to do the same thing. Abraham had to call it into reality by mixing faith with God's word.

While Abram and his wife were waiting for this child, God told Abram to count the stars at night or the sand in the daytime. Benny Hinn says, "If you start counting negatives, you will get negatives. If you see multitudes, you get multitudes. You must see it. Without seeing it, you will never get it."[15] In other words, the sick person must not see himself as being sick, but must see himself as being well. The Bible records in Romans 4:17-22 that Abraham was fully persuaded that God would do what He had promised. The way he became fully persuaded was by calling those things which were not yet manifested as though they already were.

Faith Visualization is Biblical

Some Christians are afraid of visualization, but faith visualization is biblical. It is calling those things that be not as though they were. Abraham didn't look at the impossibilities; he looked at God and received the promise. Visualization is simply a human process of focusing our attention and building our faith. Jesus made clay with his saliva and placed it on the eyes of the blind man before he was healed. The blind man could feel the clay on his eyes, and this encouraged his faith. Christ was simply helping the man to have more faith. Velmer Gardner suggests "As hands are laid upon you for healing, let your faith arise and touch God until you can see by faith that in reality it is the hands of Jesus upon you."[16]

Benny Hinn admonishes: "Speak faith images to your sickness. If you are in a wheel chair, see yourself out of it. If you have cancer, see yourself free of it. Consider not the things around you."[17] If a person has cancer, he must realize that the cancer cell is a weak, confused cell.[18] The sick person should picture his body's own white blood cells going into the area where the cancer is and destroying it. White blood cells are strong and aggressive.[19] One should picture the cancer shrinking until it is gone. He must see himself as being well, free of disease and full of energy.

Picturing the Disease on Jesus

A sick person may get well by simply picturing Jesus on the cross with his disease. Francis Hunter asks, "Can you imagine all of the cerebral palsy from the first man to the last man on the body of Jesus? See Him with all the cancer in the world from the first man to the last man…Can you imagine all the brain damage in the world on Him? Can you see all the crippling diseases on Him? Millions of all kinds of diseases, all on Jesus at one time…When we begin to see our disease back on Jesus…, healing will become a reality in our lives…If you do not receive healing the first time you think you see your disease on Jesus, keep trying. Keep seeing your disease back on Jesus!"[20]

See Yourself Doing What You Would be Doing if You Were Well

The sick person must see himself doing what he would do if he were well. In *The Healing Light*, Agnes Sanford tells of praying for a little boy with a leaky heart.[21] The child's heart got better but not completely well. The child knew all about God, which frustrated Mrs. Sanford because she had had great results before in praying for children with heart problems. She realized that the child needed her to teach him how to make his knowledge of God work for the healing of his heart. She suggested to him, "Let's play a pretend game. Pretend you're a big guy going to high school, and you are on the football squad. Shut your eyes and see yourself holding the ball and running ahead of all the other fellows. Hear them say, 'Look at that guy!' The other kids will say, 'Just look at him run! Boy he's strong! I bet he's got a strong heart.' Then you say, 'Thank you, God, because that's the way it's going to be.' " She said, "Play it every night right after your prayers." Mrs. Sanford reported that a month later when she saw the child, the doctors had given him the report that his heart was perfect.

Thinking of the Part of the Body That Needs to be Healed

The sick person must also think of the part of the body that needs to be healed. Agnes Sanford writes, "See it well and perfect and shining with God's light and then give thanks that this is being accomplished."[22] She suggests that when a person finds himself thinking, "One of my headaches is coming on," he should correct that thought with the words, "Whose headache?" We should say, "God's light shines within me and God doesn't have headaches." Then we should rejoice in the Lord and give thanks. When a person begins thinking, "I am getting the flu," he must see his nose and throat and chest filling with God's light. If there are any germs there, he must see them as being destroyed immediately. Then he should rejoice saying. "I give thanks, Oh Lord, for thy life within me, recreating all immune passages in perfect health."[23]

Mrs. Sanford also has some suggestions for the one who is so weak he does not have the strength to get up and work.[24] She reminds us that God's strength is made perfect in our weakness. For example, Mrs. Sanford tells of a lady who was in great pain and had an incurable disease. The woman said, "The pain is great, but God said get up and work." She took one step and then rested. She began to peel potatoes and said, "I am peeling this potato in the strength of almighty God. I can't exhaust His strength, because He is inexhaustible. So I will get this potato peeled and for that, oh Lord, I do thank you." Then she rested, and then she did another. The woman recovered.

Seeing the Treatment Aiding Healing

In their book *Getting Well Again*, the Simontons offer suggestions to those who must receive special treatments for their disease. They suggest that if a person is receiving radiation treatments, he should picture it as being a beam made up of millions of bullets of energy hitting any cells in its path. "The normal cells are able to repair any damage that is done, but the cancerous cells cannot because they are weak...If you are receiving chemotherapy, picture that drug coming into your body and entering the bloodstream. Picture the drug acting like a poison. The normal cells are intelligent and strong and don't take up the poison so readily. But the cancer cell is a weak cell so it takes very little to kill it. It absorbs the poison, dies, and is flushed out of your body."[25] They then suggest, "Picture your body's own white blood cells coming into the area where the cancer is, recognizing the abnormal cells, and destroying them. There is a vast army of white blood cells. They are very strong and aggressive. They are also very smart. There is no contest between them and the cancer cells; they will win the battle."[26] They also suggest: "Picture the cancer shrinking. See the dead cells being carried away by the white blood cells and being flushed from your body through the liver and kidneys and eliminated in the urine and stool."[27] For those experiencing pain in the body, they suggest, "Picture the army of white blood cells flowing into that area and soothing the pain. Whatever the problem, give your body the command to heal itself. Visualize your body becoming well. Imagine yourself well, free of disease, full of energy."[28]

Biblical Visualization Will Work for all Diseases

The same processes that work for cancer will work for other diseases. The Simontons remind us that for any disease, you can "picture your body's natural defenses and natural processes eliminating the source of the ailment or pain."[29] When I used this type of visualization, I usually saw the disease on Jesus in the background while I was visualizing the other scenes.

Guideline for Visualization

Francis Hunter warns: "This is a spiritual and supernatural dimension that can be most rewarding; however, do not visualize something that you can't line up with

God's word. Line it up with God's word and watch it come to pass."[30] Then, what you see is what you get.

Goal Setting

Goal setting is a must. Carl and Stephanie Simonton, in their *Getting Well Again*, write, "On receiving a cancer diagnosis, there is a tendency to begin living life tentatively and conditionally. Frequently people withdraw from relationships or refuse to make commitments."[31] This establishes the negative expectancy of death rather than healing. The Simontons say, "Goals are important in getting well and in maintaining a high quality of life...The will to live is strengthened."[32] A sick person should set some short-term as well as some long-term goals. Goal setting prepares a person both emotionally and spiritually to act out his commitment to regaining his health. By setting goals he is saying that he expects to recover. Setting goals affirms that God and the one who is sick are once again in charge of the person's life rather than satan and sickness.

For some, asking the question, "What do I want out of life?" is a very difficult question. After a crisis illness, one should decide what he wants to be doing in a week, a month, a year, five years, ten years. Ask questions as, "What do I want to do today that makes it worth getting out of bed for? What do I want to have accomplished in five years that makes it worth the effort?" These are the questions that will make the difference in whether you live or die.

The warrior should set goals in every area of his life. He should set physical goals for his health. He should set spiritual goals. He should set family goals. He should set goals concerning his church and community. Every area of life at this particular time needs goals.

Make goals specific and measurable. Set a time period on them. Write them down. If you would like to learn to play the piano, write down the plan for doing this. Write down the day on which you will contact a teacher, schedule lesson time and practice time. Instead of saying, "I want to be more loving," schedule time on your calendar to spend with family members or friends. If you wish to write a book, outline your plan for doing it. Do not depend on others. Focus on what you can do rather than what others will do. Assume responsibility for your own actions.

Write out two one-month goals, two three-month goals, two six-month goals, two one-year goals, and two five-year goals. Don't let anything stop you!

Dealing With Negative People

Staying away from negative people is essential for a person who is warring to be healed. Norvel Hayes warns, "Friends and relatives can kill a person who is trying to get well."[33] Pat Hayes, who had cancer several times and was healed, urges, "Don't ever leave a loved one who needs a miracle in the hands of someone who is full of doubt and unbelief."[34] Whenever her husband was leaving her for any long length of time, he made sure there were two women there who would stand over her bedside quoting the Word of God and commanding health into her body. She further said, "If it takes not allowing relatives and friends in the room, do it."[35]

It often becomes necessary to tune out best friends who feel compelled to tell about someone they knew who died of the disease. The sick person must learn to tune this out and disregard such information. When I was fighting for my life, I once found in my mailbox a large envelope filled with literature sent to my family. When I opened it, I discovered that a well-intentioned group had sent several booklets on how a family copes when the mother dies of breast cancer. I learned not to be dissuaded by such attacks.

The Importance of Words

The sick person must not speak idle words. Pat Hayes says, "If you want to be healed, you must get your tongue straightened out."[36] A person who is sick must be careful not to annul his faith by wrong conversation. Osborn says, "You cannot talk sickness and disease and walk in health. You cannot talk about disease and pains, complaining about your troubles and obtaining everybody's sympathy and be healed."[37] Charles Capps says, "I am convinced from my study of the word of God that your own words can change your immune system for better or worse. The words you speak are vital to your health and well being. I believe there are some diseases that will never be cured unless people learn to speak the language of health that the body understands."[38] This subject will be discussed in greater detail in Chapter 4.

Dealing with Fear

When a person is weak and sick, fear often overwhelms him. Satan will torment the person with the doctor's words, "You have only a few weeks to live...a few weeks to live...a few weeks to live." He uses pain and then says, "You're going to die," or "You will be buried in that dress." Fear can cause a person's mind to become subjective. John G. Lake says, "When you are full of fear, your pores will absorb everything around you. You are drawing into yourself what is around you. That is the way people absorb disease."[39]

When a person has cancer, the terrors by night become real. Dodie Osteen expressed it this way: "The devil bombarded my mind with every kind of fear imaginable, especially when everybody was asleep and I lay awake hurting. Pain—intense, unbearable pain—came against my body, most of it demonic, just to try my faith. I fought so hard in the middle of the night! That is when the devil's thoughts would play on my mind...I felt like I had battle fatigue."[40] This is a normal reaction for people who have been told about a life-threatening disease. Women who have gone through breast cancer and surgery have told the writer of horrible nightmares such as demons chasing them. But the psalmist said, "Thou shalt not be afraid for the terror by night" (Ps. 91:5).

Doctors' reports must be dealt with. To continue hearing all the possible things that could happen is to live in fear. The sick person must tune out the pessimistic prognosis of the doctor and tune into the Word of God. When asked what the doctor is reporting, it is better to answer with what the Lord is reporting.

Attacking Fear With Authority

The sick person must learn to treat sickness as the thing that it is: something from hell that is trying to attach itself to you. You must resist it. Norvel Hayes says, "When you get up in the morning and that cancer tries to attack, say 'No, you don't, no you don't, no you don't, cancer. I told you last night you are dead. In Jesus name, I said stop. Jesus is healing me now.' You must treat sickness like a mad dog and kick it out of your house. Do not pamper sickness. Treat it like a devil."[41] He continues, "Talk to that mountain sickness. Take authority over it. Say, 'In Jesus name come out. Go from me. I command my body to be normal.' Do it every day."[42]

The Warrior's Nutrition

Of vital importance is the warrior's eating habits, and the Bible has a great deal to say about that subject. We could live a longer, healthier, and happier life if we ate the healing foods described in the Bible, which is one of the earliest sources for knowledge about good health. Carlson Wade states in *Bible Healing Foods*: "As a diet reference book, the Bible is probably the most valuable volume in the world today."[43] He says, "They saw how youthfulness could be extended through a <u>diet based mainly on fruits, vegetables, and grains.</u>"[44]

Wholegrain bread

The Bible even gives a recipe for nutritious bread. "Come home with me and eat bread," says the prophet of Bethel in First Kings 13:15. In Bible days they ate the kind of wholegrain bread that we know today to be a good source of fiber and nutrition. Ezekiel 4:9 gives this recipe: "Wheat, barley, beans, lentiles, millet, and fitches." Most health food stores carry "Ezekiel bread," which has this statement on the wrapper: "Combining grains with legumes creates a complete protein that more closely resembles that in meat, milk or eggs. Sprouting makes this protein easier for the body to use."[45] It further states: "The protein quality found in this bread is so that it is 84.3 percent as efficient as the highest recognized source of protein, containing all eight of the essential amino acids."[46]

God's Instructions Concerning Meat

The advisability of eating beans and peas as an alternative to meat is emphasized in Daniel 1:12. Even modern science has recognized that these high-fiber foods can be lifesavers and advises us to keep them in our diets.

Concerning what meats we should or shouldn't eat, God gave clear instruction. He told Moses and Aaron that it was permissible to eat meat only if it came from an animal that chewed its cud, was cloven-footed, and parted its hoof (Lev. 11:1-3). Wade says, "This category includes cattle, sheep and lambs. Swine were taboo because they did not meet these requirements, were carriers of parasites, and sources of unhealthy animal fats."[47] Today, nutritionists by and large agree with the biblical view that everyone is better off cutting down on their consumption of red meat and replacing it with poultry, seafood, and vegetable sources of protein. In several places the writers of the Bible also recommended the people of God reduce their intake of fat (see Lev. 3:17; Lev. 7:23; Is. 66:3).

The ancient Israelites only ate fish that had fins and scales (Lev. 11:9-12). All other seafood, such as shellfish, were taboo. Wade says, "These species were scavengers, ingesting pollution near the shoreline, and they could carry infectious diseases."[48] Wade further says, "Popular seafoods in Biblical times included mackerel, salmon, bluefish, mullet, trout, sablefish, shad, butterfish, and pompano."[49]

Fruits and Vegetables

God put fruits and vegetables on the earth for the health of His people. He even took care of the Israelites in Egypt. While there, they ate such immune-boosting, cholesterol-melting foods as cucumbers, melons, onions, and garlic (Num. 11:5).

The high-protein and high-fiber fare of Jacob's pottage was another source of strength (Gen. 25:29-34). It consisted of red lentils and onions with garlic and some grains.

Dr. Bernie Siegel reports that of all his cancer patients, the ones who are vegetarians have the longest survival rates.[50] The reason for this is that the foods we put in our bodies determine the health of every cell and organ. In his book *Reversing Heart Disease,* Dr. Julian Whitaker states: "Every major killer disease of Americans—heart disease, cancer, high blood pressure, diabetes—is increased by excessive amounts of meat and animal protein, and decreased when animal protein foods are replaced with vegetable foods."[51]

The Power of Juicing

Jay Kordich, in his book *The Juiceman's Power of Juicing,* says, "The human body needs live food to build live cells. By live foods I mean uncooked fruits and vegetables. Other foods, such as nuts, grains, seeds, and legumes are live foods too. All come directly from the soil and are not first processed by another animal, as are meat, poultry, and fish. For this reason, I consider them live—and full of life."[52]

Kordich recommends that to get the most benefit from fruits and vegetables, we should juice them. He says, "One cup of carrot juice contains the equivalent nutrition of four cups of raw, chopped carrots. Juice contains about 95% of the food value of the fruit or the vegetable. Made fresh and consumed on the spot, juice instantly releases nourishment to the body through the blood stream. In the process, the body receives the necessary vitamin and mineral nutrients."[53] Incorporating juice into one's life does much for him. Kordich maintains, "The abundance of live, uncooked foods flushes your body of toxins, leaving you feeling refreshed, energized, and relaxed all at the same time. The pure foods make your skin glow, your hair shine, your breath fresh, and your entire system so regulated you will not have to give it another thought."[54]

The Juiceman also recommends juicing for serious ailments. Concerning cancer he writes, "Fruits and vegetables with high concentrations of beta carotene may help prevent certain types of cancer. These include apricots and cantaloupe in the fruit category; carrots, broccoli, sweet potatoes, and leafy greens as the main vegetables. Cruciferous vegetables such as cauliflower and cabbage can also be protective against many cancers."[55] For heart disease Kordich recommends pure orange juice because it strengthens the blood vessels and capillaries.[56] He also recommends juices with beets in them and juices containing green juice. For prostate problems he recommends cranberry juice as well as watermelon juice.[57] I personally recommend that any person who is dealing with serious health problems get a juicer and a good juice recipe book.

In his book, *A Cancer Therapy*, Dr. Max Gerson, one of the preeminent geniuses in medical history, gave a recipe for green juice that has helped many cancer patients. He suggests procuring as many of these kinds of leaves as possible and juicing them: "lettuce, red cabbage, beet tops, Swiss chard, escarole, endives, romaine, green pepper, watercress. Add one medium apple for each glass."[58] For salads Gerson recommends the following raw fruits and vegetables: apples and carrots, lettuce, chicory, watercress, tomatoes, escarole, cauliflower, romaine, radishes, scallions, endives, celery, chives, and green peppers.[59]

Dark green vegetables are especially good for the body. Dr. Yoshihide Hagiwara says, "The creative power of dark green leaves has always been the nutrient source of life and well-being for the human body."[60] Dr. Hagiwara researched all the green leaves and decided that green barley was the most powerful of all of them for aiding in the healing of the human body. He claims that the miracle of green barley is that it fosters the one true healing miracle, the body's ability to cure itself.[61]

Honey Recommended in the Bible

In Proverbs 24:13, Solomon advises: "My son, eat thou honey, because it is good." Honey was said to keep one mentally keen and provide physical strength. Moses ate honey in the fields. The Promised Land was called a land of "milk and honey." Today, many nutritionists suggest that we use honey as a sweetener rather than sugar.

Speaking in Tongues

Speaking in tongues is another highly powerful method of healing for the warrior. Paul said, "He that speaketh in an unknown tongue edifieth himself" (1 Cor. 14:4a). John Sherrill wrote, "The thing that happens is just what Paul said would happen: I am built up, am given joy, courage, peace, the sense of God's presence."[62] Sometimes a sick person is too weak to pray. That is when he can say, "Holy Spirit, you pray for me." Francis McNutt, a former Catholic priest, said, "Those who pray in tongues, when they are not sure precisely what to pray for, turn the prayer over to the Spirit, believing that...the Spirit can express our plea in a way that we could never put into words."[63] He testifies, "Often when I have been pressed for time, with a crowd waiting for prayer and no chance to speak to each one, I have simply gone from one person to another, laying my hands on their heads or shoulders, praying in tongues about 30 seconds for each person...In this way many have been healed."[64]

The Healing Power of Laughter

"A major factor in staying healthy is staying happy," says Dr. Patrick Quillin in *Healing Nutrients*.[65] A great incentive to being joyful and happy is found in Proverbs 17:22: "A merry heart doeth good like a medicine." Norman Cousins was stricken with an incurable disease and laughed himself to health.[66] This is an important ingredient in the process of getting well again.

The Necessity of Forgiveness

Some people do not get healed because they refuse to forgive a person who has wounded them. When warring for healing, the sick person must not hold on to any feelings of bitterness or anger. The stakes are too high. Even though he may feel that his feelings are justified, he may not get healed until he forgives the person who has wronged him. Agnes Sanford suggests, "Let us see in our minds the picture of Jesus Christ and then see the other person, placing the picture of the one we would forgive upon the picture of Christ. Having done this, we say to the one whom we would learn to like, 'I forgive you in the name of Jesus Christ, and I give thanks to God because you are now forgiven. Amen.' And we remember that 'amen' means 'so be it,' and is therefore a command sent forth in the name of Christ."[67] She further exhorts, "Having once accomplished a forgiveness...we must never question it, lest we stop the work that He is doing through us. Having said, 'I give thanks that so and so is forgiven,' we must keep on giving thanks that this is so. We must trust the actual working of God through us, and must not be misled by our own unruly feelings."[68] Forgiveness must be received from God and given to others.

The Power of Fasting

So often we cry out, "O God, raise up men and women who can lay hands on the sick and they will recover." But we quickly end our prayers because we are hungry and everyone must eat before the meal gets cold. The practice of fasting while praying has been lost. The enemy has kept us from fasting because he does not want us to have the increased power we receive from fasting.

In Matthew 17:14-21, we read about a man who had brought his demon-possessed son to the Lord. He had previously brought him to the disciples, but they could not help the boy or his father. When Jesus rebuked the devil, he departed and the child was cured. The disciples asked, "Why could we not do that?" Jesus' answer was this: "This kind goeth not out but by prayer and fasting." Only those who are willing to learn how to effectively pray and fast and seek the face of God will experience the power of God manifested in this way. Fasting gets results.

In addition, fasting is good for our health because it cleanses the body. Jay Kordich says, "My body works hard twenty-four hours a day, six days a week; I view fasting as its day off. During this day the body cleanses, purifies, and essentially resurrects itself. During the fast, the system flushes out the liver, kidneys, and bladder and eliminates toxins."[69]

Watching What Jesus is Doing

Today's Christian is called to do greater works than Jesus did (Jn. 14:12). The secret of Christ's miraculous ministry was His intimate relationship with His Father. He acted only on what He saw the Father doing (Jn. 5:17-21). He did nothing on His own initiative. We, too, can work the works of God and do these "greater works" if we will only discover the relationship Jesus had with the Father. John Wimber says, "The ability to hear what God is saying, to see what God is doing, and to move in the realm of the miraculous comes as an individual develops the same intimacy with and dependence upon the Father."[70]

Anyone who will watch what God is doing can work the miraculous and bring healing and good health to the sick. After T.L. Osborne came home from India utterly defeated, he went to a meeting conducted by William Branham, which became the turning point in his life and ministry. He wrote, "As I watched Brother Branham minister to the sick, I was especially captivated by the deliverance of a little deaf-mute girl over whom he had prayed this: 'Thou deaf and dumb spirit, I adjure thee in Jesus' name, leave the child.' When he snapped his fingers, the girl heard and spoke perfectly. When I witnessed this there seemed to be a thousand voices speaking to me at once all in one accord saying over and over, 'You can do that.' "[71] Powerfully influenced by what he saw and strengthened by a visitation from Jesus, Osborne began to minister, ultimately traveling all over the world with his wife, Daisy, and bringing healing to thousands. We, too, can do that.

We understand that the person who is warring for healing is God's main weapon of warfare. In Jeremiah 31:20 God tells us, "You are my war club, my weapon for battle—with you I shatter nations, with you I destroy kingdoms." Though you may have been attacked with some disease, this can be a time of tremendous spiritual growth. Not only will you be healed, but you will bring healing to a world that is under attack by the devil. We declare war on sickness. Devil, back off. We are God's property!

Warfare Healing Principles

- The very life style of the warrior is a weapon.

- The priority of the sick person must be getting well.

- You may have to be feisty to get healed.

- State aloud your plan to live and declare the works of God.

- The sick person must understand where and why the battle is coming.

- You must not get it into your mind that God is chastening you.

- God has the Word and the Holy Spirit to instruct His children, not sickness.

- Know your authority and surround yourself with people who know their authority.

- Satan Has no right to put on you what God put on Jesus.

- God has no favorites.

- See yourself well.

- Call those things that be not as though they were.

- Set goals for one month, two months, three months, six months, one year, five years.

- Don't leave a loved one who needs a miracle in the hands of someone who is full of doubt and un-belief.

- Get your tongue straightened out.

- Speak the language of health.

- Your words can change your immune system.

- F E A R is False Evidence Appearing Real.

- The body needs live foods to build live cells.

- A merry heart doeth good like a medicine.

- We war by forgiving.

- Fasting gets results.

- Those who will watch what God is doing can work the miraculous and bring health and healing to the sick.

Endnotes

1. Dr. Bernie Siegel, *Peace, Love and Healing* (New York: Harper and Row, 1990), p. 27.

2. Terry Law, Necessity of Faith, Tape 1, Terry Law Ministries, 1990.

3. Frank Hammond, *The Saints at War* (Plainview, TX: Children Bread, 1990), p. 13.

4. Joyce Boisseau, *You Can Live in Divine Health* (Lancaster, PA: Starburst Publishers, 1983), p. 22.

5. T.L. Osborn, *Healing the Sick* (Tulsa, OK: Harrison House, Inc., 1951), p. 105.

6. Ibid., p. 106.

7. Ibid., p. 107.

8. Ibid., p. 13.

9. E.W. Kenyon, *Jesus the Healer* (Lynwood, WA: Kenyon's Gospel Publishing Society, 1968), p. 11.

10. Ibid., p. 44.

11. Ibid.

12. Lillian Yeoman, *Balm of Gilead* (Springfield, MO: Gospel Publishing House, 1936), p. 46.

13. Ibid.

14. Charles Capps, *God's Creative Power for Healing* (Tulsa, OK: Harrison House, nd), pp. 5-6.

15. Benny Hinn, *Healing*, Tape 5.

16. Velmer Garder, *Healing for You* (Springfield, MO: Velmer Gardner Ministries, 1952), p. 22.

17. Benny Hinn, *Divine Healing*, Tape 5.

18. O. Carl and Stephanie Simontons, *Getting Well Again* (New York: Bantam Books, 1980), p. 155.

19. Ibid.

20. Frances Hunter, *To Heal the Sick* (Kingwood, TX: Hunter Books, 1983), p. 85.

21. Agnes Sanford, *The Healing Light* (NJ: Logos, 1947), p. 16.

22. Agnes Sanford, p. 26.

23. Ibid., pp. 26-27.

24. Ibid., p. 41.

25. Simontons, p. 144.

26. Ibid.

27. Ibid.

28. Ibid., p. 145.

29. Ibid., p. 146.

30. Hunter, p. 92.

31. Simontons, p. 106.

32. Ibid.

33. Norvel Hayes, *How to Live and Not Die*, Tape 3.

34. Pat Hayes, Testimony on tape.

35. Ibid.

36. Pat Hayes, Testimony on tape.

37. Osborn, p. 191.

38. Capps, p. 7.

39. John G. Lake, *Sermons on Dominion over Demons, Disease, and Death* (Dallas: Christ for the Nations, 1940), p. 104.

40. Dodie Osteen, *Healed of Cancer* (Tulsa, OK: Harrison House, 1986), p. 28.

41. Norvell Hayes, *How to Live and Not Die*, Tape 3.

42. Ibid.

43. Carlson Wade, *Bible Healing Foods* (New York: Globe Communications, 1988), p. 2.

44. Ibid.

45. Wrapper on Ezekiel Bread bought at health food store.

46. Ibid.

47. Wade, p. 5

48. Ibid.

49. Ibid., p. 6.

50. Dr. Bernie Siegel, Tape.

51. Dr. Julian Whitaker, *Reversing Heart Disease* (New York: Warner Books, 1985), p. 118.

52. Jay Kordich, *The Juiceman's Power of Juicing* (New York: William Morris and Company, 1992), p. 26.

53. Kordich, p. 27.

54. Ibid., p. 29.

55. Ibid., p. 233.

56. Ibid., p. 234.

57. Ibid., p. 235.

58. Dr. Max Gerson, *A Cancer Therapy* (Bonita, CA: Gerson Institute, 1958), p. 241.

59. Ibid., p. 242.

60. Hoshihide Hagiwara, *Green Barley Essence* (New Canaan, CT: Keats Publishing, Inc., 1986), p. 1.

61. Ibid., p. 13.

62. John Sherrill, *They Speak With Other Tongues* (New York: McGraw Hill, 1964), p. 83.

63. Francis McNutt, *Healing* (Notre Dame, IN: Ave Maria Press, 1974), p. 207.

64. Ibid.

65. Dr. Patrick Quillin, *Healing Nutrients* (Chicago: Contemporary Books, 1987), p. 154.

66. Video Tape of story of Norman Cousins.

67. Sanford, pp. 58-59.

68. Sanford, p. 59.

69. Kordich, p. 251.

70. John Wimber, *Healing Clinic Notes* (Pasadena, CA: Fuller Seminary, 1988), p. 9.05.

71. David Edwin Harrell, *All Things are Possible* (Bloomington, IN: Indiana University Press, 1975), p. 64.

Part Two

The Battle Plan

Chapter Three

The Mighty Warheads: The Word, the Name, and the Blood

"For the weapons of our warfare are mighty through God to the pulling down of strongholds" (2 Cor. 10:4). Sickness is a stronghold. Symptoms become strongholds. If we focus our spiritual eyes on symptoms, we can be overcome by the power they exert. But we have weapons that will pull down these strongholds.

There are three powerful weapons God has given to every believer. They are the Word of God, the name of Jesus, and the blood of Jesus. These are the warheads. Terry Law says, "The power for explosion, the power for destruction, is in the warhead."[1] The key is to get them to the point of attack. This means we must have missiles to carry each warhead to its target. Tarry Law refers to them as rockets, saying, "If we were to launch a rocket that did not carry a warhead, it would create a minor explosion when it hit the ground. However, if that rocket carried a warhead, it would obliterate an entire city and much of the surrounding countryside. The power for destruction is in the warhead and not in the rocket."[2]

The missiles that propel our powerful spiritual warheads are praise, worship, prayer, confession, resistance, binding and loosing, preaching, testimony, and breaking generational curses. Let's first discuss the warheads; in the next chapter will examine the missiles.

The Word of God

It is impossible to overemphasize the power of God's Word in the life of a believer. Christ is the living Word of God; the Bible is the written Word of God. Psalm 107:20 says, "He sent His word, and healed them, and delivered them from their destructions."

The Bible is a Supernatural Book

The Word of God is a supernatural book. God guarantees to provide healing through His Word. If He has sent His Word to heal, then His Word will heal. T.L. and Daisy Osborne have preached in countries around the world, laid hands upon the sick, and seen many great miracles of healing. But T.L. Osborn writes: "Among the tens of thousands who have been miraculously healed by the Lord, most of them were healed while meditating on the Bible."[3] Many have even been miraculously healed by placing the Bible under their pillows at night.

The Word is Creative

God's Word is just as effective today, just as powerful and just as creative, as when the worlds were framed by the Word of God. Ezekiel 12:25 says, "I am the Lord: I will speak, and the word that I shall speak shall come to pass." Matthew 24:35 declares, "Heaven and earth shall pass away, but my words shall not pass away." Romans 4:21 declares, "What He had promised, He was able also to perform." Luke 1:37 says, "No word from God is void of power." Jesus Christ is the same yesterday, today, and forever. He has not changed, and His word has not changed. His word is just as up-to-date as the morning newspaper.

The Word Can be Depended Upon

Regardless of our circumstances, we can depend on the Word of God. God watches over His Word to see that not one word fails. "I will hasten [stand behind or back up] my word to perform it" (Jer. 1:12b). Job said, "I know that my redeemer liveth" (Job 19:25a). He made this statement while afflicted with leprosy. His flesh was rotting off. Though he didn't feel well, he knew that he could believe God's Word. Lillian Yeoman said, "Give me knowledge every time and away with what I feel. I don't care what I feel when I know…[I] know that He is my redeemer and that He liveth; and because He lives, I live and shall live forever. I live this moment. My redeemer liveth and is doing His work—redeeming me. From what? From the curse of broken law which includes every disease that flesh is heir to. What remains but praise?"[4]

The Word Produces the Promise

T.L. Osborne says, "The creative power of God's word will create the very thing in your body that you need in order to be well and strong."[5] When believed and acted upon, any promise of God is transformed into the power of God. Osborn maintains, "Every promise of God contains the power necessary to produce what it promises, when it is believed and acted upon."[6]

The Word is Powerful When Fed Upon

Hebrews 4:12 says, "For the word of God is quick, and powerful, and sharper than any twoedged sword, piercing even to the dividing asunder of soul and spirit." The key to partaking of the healing life and energy in the Word is feeding on it until it penetrates into your spirit. There it will deposit its healing life and energy.

Faith is Built on the Word of God

Real faith is built on the Word of God. Paul wrote, "Faith cometh by hearing, and hearing by the word of God" (Rom. 10:17). The Word of God is actually God speaking to us. It is God-breathed, God-inspired, and God-indwelt. Kenneth Hagin advises, "Wrap yourself up in it."[7] Use it! Matthew 15:13 became a "rhema" to me during my crisis with cancer: "Every plant, which my heavenly Father hath not planted, shall be rooted up." A "rhema" is a Spirit-inspired word from the written "logos" that brings life, power, and faith to perform and fulfill it. It is a personal word from the Bible. This Scripture became that to me.

The Word Must Be Personal

The Word of God must become personal. Kenneth Hagin says,"If God's Word says it's true, then it's true. It is mine, and I have it now. I have it now even though I can't see it because God cannot lie."[8]

The Word is More Powerful Than Prayers of Other People

The Word is more powerful than the prayers of other people. When a person gets himself into agreement with God through His Word, he can expect a miracle. Many people rush from one meeting to another, hoping that some well-known person will pray the prayer of faith for them. But if they would simply get into the Word of God, healing would become a reality. The reason some do not keep their healing is because their faith is grounded in the prayers of other people rather than the Word of God.

Giving Attention to God's Word Brings Healing

Giving complete attention to God's Word brings the miracle of healing. Proverbs 4:20-22 says, "My son, attend to my words; incline thine ear unto my sayings. Let them not depart from thine eyes; keep them in the midst of thine heart. For they are life unto those that find them, and health to all their flesh." A sick person must attend to the Word more carefully than he would attend to a child.

Incline thine ear. Listen to the Word of God. John Osteen says, "Faith cometh by hearing and hearing and hearing."[9] One of the most successful ways of getting the Word into one's spirit is to listen to tapes of healing Scriptures all night long.

Let them not depart from thine eyes. Read the Words of healing over and over. A person who is sick should not let a day go by without reading the healing Scriptures God has given. Hagin says, "Many people fail because they allow the Word of God to depart from before their eyes. Instead of seeing themselves as God's word says they are, they keep looking at the wrong things— at the conditions, at the symptoms, at themselves—and so they walk in unbelief and destroy the effects of their faith."[10]

Keep them in the midst of thine heart. Memorize the healing Scriptures. Find the Scriptures that fit your case; mark them in the Bible; go to surgery with the references written on your hand; claim them. Norvel Hayes declares, "It doesn't take many Scriptures to get your healing. One Scripture verse can bring your healing miracle."[11] Find those verses that are a rhema to you.

The Word Becomes Health to Sick Flesh

The Word will actually become life to the sick person. The Word of God can keep you from dying when it looks like all hope is gone. It will become health to all your flesh—cancerous flesh, arthritic flesh, heart attack flesh, diabetic flesh.

The Word is Medicine

The Hebrew word translated *health* in Proverbs 4:22 means medicine. In other words, God's Word is medicine to all our flesh. There are several parallels between God's medicine and natural medicine. God's word is a healing agent just as natural medicine is a healing agent or catalyst to healing. The medicine itself contains the capacity to produce healing. God's Word contains inherent within it the capacity, the energy, the ability, the nature to effect healing in your body.

The Word is literally a painkiller. Solomon declares, "A bundle of myrrh is my well-beloved unto me; He shall sleep all night betwixt my breasts" (Song 1:13). Myrrh is an analgesic, which in the Old Testament times was given to sick people to kill the pain. When Jesus was being crucified, He was offered myrrh to kill the pain, but refused because He did not want to die without pain. The Bible is our painkiller. The Song of Solomon refers to Jesus (the living Word) as myrrh. The written Word will be our painkiller if we will receive it.

Medicine is no respecter of persons. However, medicine is to be taken no matter how you feel. The Word of God is likewise truth no matter how you feel.

Medicine must be taken according to directions to be effective. Some medicine is to be taken internally. It would not help to rub it on the body. To take it several times a week when the directions say three times a day will produce only limited results. It has to be taken according to directions. So it is with God's medicine. The directions are found in Proverbs 4:20-21. We must attend to the Word; we must give careful attention to it. We must put everything else out of our minds and concentrate all our faculties on the Word.

Medicine takes time to work. People do not take one dose and expect immediate results. They are patient with it. We must do the same with the Word.

The Word of God must be acted upon; it must be obeyed. In the *Word Bible Helps*, Kenneth Hagin tells of his being bedfast at the age of fifteen. He was almost completely paralyzed. Five doctors were called in on his case and they all agreed that there was absolutely no hope for him. As far as medical science knew, no one in his condition had ever lived past the age of sixteen. But he loved God and fought death with every fiber of his being. While he was in bed, he read the Word constantly. He had attempted to act on the Word, but still did not receive his healing. On the second Tuesday of August, 1934, after being sick for sixteen months, he prayed, "Dear Lord Jesus, when you were here on earth, you said in Mark 11:24, 'What things soever ye desire, when ye pray, believe that ye receive them, and ye shall have them.' Dear Lord Jesus, I desire to be healed. You said, 'when you pray.' I have prayed. Dear Lord Jesus, if you stood here by my bedside in the flesh and if you were to say, son, the trouble with you is you're not believing, I would have to reply to you, Dear Lord Jesus, you are lying about it—I do believe." God spoke to him deep within. "Yes, you believe all right—as far as you know—but the last clause of this verse of Scripture is, believe that ye receive them and ye shall have them." Then Hagin saw it. It was just as if someone had turned a light on inside of him. He cried,"Dear Lord Jesus, I see it! I see it! I have to believe I receive my healing. I have to believe I receive healing for my heart while my heart is still not beating right. I receive healing for my paralysis even though I am paralyzed from a natural standpoint. If I believe I receive healing, then I have it." He said, "I had wanted to receive my healing first, and then believe it." After receiving this revelation of God's Word, he began to praise the Lord, "Thank you, God, I am healed."

Then God spoke and said, "But well people don't have any business in bed. They need to be up." He said, "I didn't look any better, and I didn't feel any better. Physically, I had no feeling from my waist down. I was still partially paralyzed having only about two-thirds use of the upper part of my body. But I pushed myself to a sitting position and pulled my knees up against my chest. Then I made an effort to twist my body and pushed my feet off the bed. I grabbed hold of the bed-post at the foot of the bed and pulled myself off the bed.

My feet fell on the floor like chunks of wood. Although I couldn't feel them, I could see them down there on the floor." Thoughts began to penetrate his mind as fast as machine gun bullets: "You can't walk. You're not healed. You're going to fall right on the floor, and you'll just have to lie there." He held on to the bedpost and lifted one hand a little and said, "Thank God, I'm healed. I want to declare it in the presence of almighty God, the Lord Jesus Christ, the angels in Heaven and in the presence of the devil and evil spirits, that the Word of God is true, and I believe I am healed. I believe it." He said the room seemed to be spinning. He shut his eyes and said again, "Thank God, according to the Word, I am healed." Then he felt a warm glow dropping on his head. He said, "It seemed to flow down over me as if a jar of warm honey had been poured over my head. It ran down my whole body. When it reached my waist, feeling began to return to the lower part of my body. At first the pain was excruciating, but when you haven't had any feelings at all for so long, it even feels good to hurt. Then I felt normal. The paralysis was gone." He said, "I'm going to walk now," and he did. It took some time to build his muscles back up from so many months of inactivity, but he started walking that day.[12]

We can see from the foregoing study that the Word of God must abide within the sick person concerning his healing. We have a covenant with God that includes divine healing. Hosea said, "My people are destroyed for lack of knowledge" (Hos. 4:6). Christians have allowed disease to kill them while God's Word has been saying, "By His stripes ye are healed (1 Pet. 2:24). Christians are helpless in the face of satan and disease without the Word of God living in them. The seed of the Word concerning healing must be planted in the warrior so that he can successfully reap the healing harvest.

We see then that a person must act on the Word. After reading the Word, you act on it while you can still see the swelling, feel the pain, and are conscious of the symptoms. Believe what God said right then in the face of all contrary sense knowledge. Act on the Word and stand solidly. The symptoms cry out, "You are not healed." The Word of God, which cannot lie, says, "By His stripes ye are healed." Stand with the Word of God. Agree with it. Read the Word, talk the Word, confess the Word, and the Word will become a very part of you.

The Name of Jesus

"And whatsoever ye ask in My name, that will I do" (Jn. 14:13a). "Whatsoever ye shall ask the Father in My name, He will give it you" (Jn. 16:23). According to these Scriptures, we have the right to ask the Father for healing in the name of Jesus.

There is Power in the Name

Philippians 2:9-10 says, "God also hath highly exalted Him, and given Him a name which is above every name: that at the name of Jesus every knee should bow, of things in heaven [angels], and things in earth [men], and things under the earth [demons]." Beings in all three worlds bow at the name of Jesus. That name holds dominion over satan and his entire kingdom. That name holds power over sickness and disease. All that Jesus was, His name is. That name has lost none of its power.

Jesus Gave Us the Power of Attorney

Jesus gave His followers the legal right to use His name. All the power and all the authority that was in Jesus in the flesh is now available to us in His name. He gave His name to the Church. Jesus defeated the devil and all of hell, and stands before the three worlds— Heaven, Earth, and hell—as the undisputed victor over man's ancient destroyer. Here is a model for how we ought to pray: "Father, Jesus is there at your right hand and has given us the power of attorney to carry out your will on earth. So here is my sickness. I ask you in His name to heal it." It's up to us to enforce this authority in our lives. A sick Christian has authority to speak directly to his sickness and say, "Sickness, I resist you. In the name of Jesus Christ, leave my body." He does not have to wait for God to do it. God gave us the power of attorney to do it in His name.

The Early Church Used the Name of Jesus to Heal

The early Church knew what they had—and they used it. Peter and John said to the crippled man, "Silver and gold have I none; but such as I have give I thee: In the name of Jesus Christ of Nazareth rise up and walk" (Acts 3:5-6). The man immediately rose up and walked. Paul said to a demon, "I command you in the name of Jesus Christ to come out of her" (Acts 16:18). The woman was restored that very hour.

That Name Will Bring Healing Today

Smith Wigglesworth tells of six men ministering to a man who was dying from tuberculosis. They had prayed and nothing had happened. One of the six said, "There is one thing we did not try. Let us go back in and whisper the name of Jesus." While standing beside the bed, they did nothing but repeat the name of Jesus over and over. The presence of God began to fill the room and healing flowed into that dying man's body. He immediately arose, perfectly whole.[13]

Another outstanding example of the power of the name of Jesus occurred when Pat Hayes was in a coma and saw four death angels coming to get her. She said, "They were armored from head to toe. Their armor did not have a dent. They looked so shiny. They looked perfect in every way. But the moment I saw them, I knew they were not warring angels. But I recognized that they were four spirits of death coming to take me. When I began to see them, I thought, 'Lord, what am I going to do?' The still small voice spoke to me and said, 'Just use my name!' I began to speak His name, not two times, not screaming it. I spoke it one time. To the first death angel, I said, 'In the name of Jesus.' The moment that I spoke that name, the brightest, the purest, the holiest light moved over and took the place of that demon. I said it again to the second, the third, the fourth. I knew then I was home free. The battle was won. Victory was mine. I was taken off the life support the next day.[14]

Let us understand that every Christian has the legal right to use the name of Jesus for healing. E.W. Kenyon says, "The weakest son has a legal right now to all the grace, and might, and power, and blessing, and health, and healing, and life enwrapped in the Person Who bore that Name."[15] All that Jesus was, His name is and will be. That name has not lost its power and is available today.

E.W. Kenyon summarizes for us: "Healing is ours, the Name makes it available to us. That Name is ours, and in that Name is all health. Do not try; do not struggle—just use it! Use it like you use your checkbook. The money is on deposit. Healing is on deposit."[16]

The Blood of Jesus

By the blood of the passover lamb, God put a difference between the Egyptians and the Hebrews (Ex. 11:7). Just before the children of Israel left Egypt, God said to Moses, "Speak to all the congregation of Israel, saying, ...take to them every man a lamb,...[and]...kill it,...[and] take the blood, and strike it on the two side posts and on the upper door post of the houses,...[and] eat the flesh [of the lamb], ...it is the Lord's passover"

(Ex. 12:3-11). And God said, "When I see the blood, I will pass over you" (v. 13). The blood of the lamb was their sure defense. It is likewise our sure defense today.

The Israelites Were to Eat the Lamb's Flesh

Each Israelite was to eat the lamb's flesh, appropriating physical strength for his journey. T.L. Osborn reminds us, "The body of the lamb slain in Egypt, when eaten, became part of each Israelite. It became flesh of their flesh, bone of their bones, skin of their skin, body of their bodies. It was a type of the body of Jesus, who was to be slain for the world..."[17]

The Blood From the Stripes of Jesus Bought Our Healing

Our sins and sicknesses were bought with the precious blood of Jesus. The stripes Jesus received brought forth much blood, which was being shed for our healing. T.J. McCrossan translates First Peter 2:24 this way: "Who by His own self bare our sins in His own body on the tree...by whose stripes (*molopi*, bruise) ye were healed."[18] He also translates Isaiah 53:5 in the Septuagint (the Greek version of the Old Testament), this way: "But He was wounded on account of our sins and was bruised because of our iniquities: the chastisement of our peace was upon Him; and by His bruise (*to molopi autou*, by the bruise of Him) we are healed."[19] McCrossan notes that Isaiah and Peter use the singular word "bruise" or "stripe" (*molopi*) and not "bruises" or "stripes."[20] He further maintains, "The word *molops* means the mark of a blow or a bruise...The use of the dative singular here, *molopi* tells us, as clearly as language can express it, that our dear Savior's back had been so terribly scourged that no one blow could possibly be distinguished from the other. Every spot on His back was so bruised and lacerated that it was just like one great bruise...The Jews had a law that no person should be given more than 40 stripes when flogged, but the Romans had no such law, so they often scourged their victim until he bled to death."[21]

McCrossan continues to describe the scourging: "He was beaten at the pleasure of the soldiers, with the knots of rope, or plaited leathern thongs, armed at the ends with acorn shaped drops of lead, or small sharp pointed bones. In many cases not only was the back of the person scourged cut open in all directions, but even the eyes, the face, and the breast were torn, and teeth not seldom knocked out..."[22] McCrossan quotes Eusebius, the early church historian, as he describes a Roman scourging of some martyrs: "All around were horrified to see them so torn with the scourges that their very veins were laid bare, and the inner muscles and sinews, and even their very bowels were exposed."[23] On Christ's poor, bruised back they then laid the heavy cross (Jn. 9:17). McCrossan feels that much of Christ's blood was shed while receiving that awful bruise for our physical healing, the rest being reserved for our sins on the cross.[24]

For some people, simply meditating on the scourging of Jesus brings healing. Some plead or declare that blood and receive their healing.

Communion Can Be a Means of Healing

There were two things the children of Israel were to do. They were to apply the blood of the lamb and eat of the lamb's body. The death angel would then pass over them on his way to slay the firstborn of every family of the Egyptians. The blood was a type of our identification by faith with the blood of Jesus, our Lamb. "Being now justified by His blood, we shall be saved from wrath through Him" (Rom. 5:9). We partake of that same body of Christ, in type, each time we partake of the bread in the communion service. The Israelites ate the lamb's body, and when they began their journey the next day, their sicknesses vanished and their infirmities disappeared. They were physically strong and whole. God was not only their deliverer from the death angel, but also the healer of their diseases. This was a type of the body of Jesus.

During the communion service we take the bread, hold it in our hand, then eat it as a token of the body of our Lamb. Too often in churches around the world we take the cup of wine and remember the blood of Jesus which was shed for our salvation while forgetting the body that was broken for our diseases. Because the church has not properly discerned the Lord's body, many are sick among us. Osborn says,"When I eat the bread, I rejoice in the fact that my sick, weak body has been changed; that it has become bone of His bone, flesh of His flesh, and body of His body; that the life of Christ has been made manifest in my mortal flesh, that sickness no longer has power over me; that I am healed. In this way, I discern the Lord's body."[25] Osborn further advises, "Discern the body as having been beaten and lacerated with stripes—stripes by which your sicknesses were borne and you were healed—and health will be yours."[26]

We are Overcomers by the Blood

The Bible says that the endtime believers overcome the devil by the blood of the Lamb and by the word of their testimony (Rev. 12:11). Terry Law explains, "They testified to what the Word said that the Blood did for them."[27] Notice that satan accuses us before God, day and night. But the Bible says we can overcome him by the blood of the Lamb. God wants us to take authority, and He has provided us with an effective means for doing this. When the enemy tells a believer that he is going to die of a disease, the declaration of the blood can bring healing.

The Missiles

The Word of God, the name of Jesus, and the precious blood of Jesus are the spiritual weapons of our warfare. However, there are missiles that transport these warheads to the place where they can destroy the power of the enemy against the sick person. We will examine these missiles in the next chapter.

Warfare Healing Principles

- The power for healing is in the warheads—the Word, the Name, and the Blood.

- The Word of God is a supernatural book.

- God's Word in you is one of the most powerful weapons in the world.

- The Word of God is sharper than any two-edged sword.

- The creative power of God's Word will create the very thing in your body that you need to be well and strong (Osborn).

- Every promise of God contains the power necessary to produce what it promises when it is believed and acted upon (Osborn).

- The Word of God is more powerful than the prayers of other people.

- When one gets into agreement with God through His Word, he can expect a miracle.

- Faith comes by hearing and hearing and hearing.

- Memorize healing Scriptures.

- One Scripture verse can bring your healing miracle (Norvel Hayes).

- We have the power of attorney—the legal right to use the name of Jesus.

- The name of Jesus brings healing.

- Beings in all three worlds bow to the name of Jesus.

- Healing is ours, the name of Jesus makes it available to us. That name is ours, and in that name is all health. Do not try; do not struggle—just use it. Use it like you use your checkbook. The money is on deposit. Healing is on deposit (Kenyon).

- We are overcomers by declaring the blood of Jesus.

Endnotes

1. Terry Law, *The Power of Praise and Worship* (Tulsa, OK, used by permission of the Publisher: Victory House Publishers, 1985), p. 107.

2. Ibid., p. 108.

3. T.L. Osborn, *Healing the Sick* (Tulsa, OK: Harrison House, 1951), p. 11.

4. Lillian Yeoman, *Balm of Gilead* (Springfield: Gospel Publishing House, 1936), p. 18.

5. Osborn, op. cit., p. 281.

6. Ibid.

7. Kenneth Hagin, *The Word Bible Helps* (Tulsa, OK: Harrison House, Inc., 1990), p. 1126.

8. Ibid.

9. John Osteen, tape of Believers Convention in Los Angeles in 1987.

10. Kenneth Hagin, op. cit., p. 1126.

11. Norvel Hayes, *How to Live and Not Die*, Tape 3.

12. Kenneth Hagin, *Word Bible Helps*, p. 1126.

13. Smith Wigglesworth, *Ever Increasing Faith* (Springfield: Gospel Publishing House, 1924), p. 28.

14. Pat Hayes, testimony on tape.

15. E.W. Kenyon, *The Wonderful Name of Jesus* (Lynwood, WA: Kenyon's Gospel Publishing Society, 1964), p. 11.

16. Ibid., p. 28.

17. Osborn, p. 257.

18. T.J. McCrossan, op. cit., p. 25.

19. Ibid.

20. Ibid., p. 26.

21. Ibid., pp. 26-27.

22. Ibid., p. 27.

23. Ibid., p. 28.

24. Ibid.

25. Osborn, p. 264.

26. Osborn, p. 265.

27. Terry Law, *Praise and Worship*, p. 111.

Chapter Four

Launching the
Missiles of War

The power for healing is in the warheads—the Word of God, the name of Jesus, and the blood of Jesus. The missiles simply carry the warheads to their targets. God has given us several powerful missiles which we will review in this chapter.

The Praise and Worship Missile

The premise of this section is very simple: praise and worship brings us healing and deliverance. This way of healing is dynamite.

The Presence of the Lord Brings Healing

In Luke 5:17 we read that the presence of the Lord has power to heal. Praise and worship creates the doorway through which we enter into His presence to receive healing. Psalms 22:3 says, "But Thou art holy, O

Thou that inhabitest the praises of Israel." God is so pleased with the praises of His people that He comes down to fellowship with us. Once He is present with us, His presence then makes sick bodies whole. Norvel Hayes says, "When you praise the Lord, you build Him a habitation, a dwelling place."[1]

The late Kathryn Kuhlman had an unusual healing ministry that was unexplainable in human terms. Believers and unbelievers both got healed. Those who knew Kathryn Kuhlman best said that she spent hours each day caught away in worshiping and praising the Lord, whom she loved with all her being. Marilyn Hickey says, "When Kathryn walked onto a platform, she simply took her audience into that worship and praise; and the power of the Lord was present to heal."[2]

First Things First—Worship God

Norvel Hayes says, "Only after you worship and praise God, do you have a right to ask God to heal you or do anything else for you. If you don't know this, it can cost you your life."[3] He goes on to say, "But if you'll put first things first, there's no such thing as the devil killing you. He doesn't have the power to kill you, if you'll worship God."[4]

There are thousands of illustrations about people praising and worshiping God and then being healed. Don Gossett, in *Praise Avenue*, tells of a man named Jack Neville who in 1952 had been involved in a serious train wreck in Fresno. X-rays revealed that his back was badly broken. The doctors had said, "In your present condition, you probably will not make it. If you do live, you will never walk again." He felt inwardly crushed. As he was praying for God to take him home if he would never walk again, Matthew 8:17 flashed across his mind: "Himself took our infirmities." As the wonder of this truth hit him, he became transformed. "With His stripes we are healed" was no longer a worn-out phrase to him. He began to worship and praise the Lord. Finally he exercised his faith and stepped down on the floor to find that he was strong. He walked out of the hospital a healed man because of praise and worship.[5]

A Choir Led the Israeli Army

Praise, worship, and music are powerful weapons. In Second Chronicles 20 we have the story of the invasion of Israel by three armies. Jehoshaphat is king of Israel and becomes afraid when he's informed of the invasion. Instead of surrendering, however, he proclaims a fast and begins seeking the Lord. The spirit of prophecy then comes upon Jahaziel. His prophetic word outlines the battle plan that God has designed. God's plan was for the choir to lead the army into battle. Following the plan, the Levites advanced before the armies of Israel, praising and worshiping the Lord with songs. As soon as they began to sing and praise, the Lord set ambushments against the three armies of the enemy. The battle plan still works today.

Praise Shook the Jail

The Apostle Paul wrote that the weapons of our warfare are "mighty through God to the pulling down of strong holds" (2 Cor. 10:4). He had a chance to practice what he preached one night in a Philippian jail. He literally pulled down the strongholds by the power of praise. Acts 16:25 declares, "At midnight Paul and Silas prayed, and sang praises unto God." In the midst of their bondage, in the midst of the pain, they praised God. They offered a sacrifice of praise, and their prison cell—the stronghold—was shaken and they were set free.

Worship Alone and Corporately

Praise and worship can be done alone or in a group. In his book *How to Live and Not Die*, Norvel Hayes shows how to best start our day. He says, "Bring your hands out from under the covers. If you can't lift them very high, just lift them a little bit. But open up your mouth and say: 'Jesus, I love You and I thank You that my name is written in heaven. I worship You, Jesus. Thou art great, O God. There are no other gods before You. Jesus, I just want to thank You because You are my Saviour and my Healer. Thank You, Jesus, for Your divine healing power. Thank You that Your healing power is flowing through my body right now to drive out every affliction, in Jesus' name. No affliction can stay in my body. I belong to You, Jesus, and I worship You.' "[6]

Though praise and worship is a personal thing, it becomes corporate when we gather with other members of the Body of Christ. Terry Law affirms, "When praise and worship is loosed by a group, there is a tremendous amount of power generated...Because corporate praise involves the power of agreement, the power of coming into harmony, there is a tremendous spiritual energy generated."[7]

On October 25, 1992, after speaking in a church in Rochester, New York, I personally saw corporate worship bring healing. After bringing a message on divine healing, I encouraged the people to take some time to worship God. After they had worshiped and praised God for about thirty minutes, numerous people began coming to the platform to tell how they had been healed as they worshiped.

Also, during a two-week intensified seminar presented by Christian International in Santa Rosa Beach in September, 1992, many were healed during the worship time after Robert Gay had preached on the power of worship. The song of the Lord had gone forth that arthritis was being healed. I was sitting next to friends from Detroit. The man was instantly healed of arthritis in the shoulder. That same evening many others told of miracles taking place.

The Difference Between Thanksgiving, Praise, and Worship

Many Christians find themselves using the words thanksgiving, praise, and worship interchangeably. There are different meanings for the words. Terry Law explains, "Thanksgiving relates to God's deeds, what He has done. Praise relates to God's character, who He is. Worship relates directly to God's holiness."[8]

Give Thanks in the Midst of Disease

We give thanks in the midst of disease by saying, "By His stripes we are healed" (1 Pet. 2:24). We give thanks that He took our infirmities and bore our sicknesses (Mt. 8:17). I like to give thanks according to Exodus 15:26, thanking Him for being the God that healeth me. We should thank God for answering satan's attack. Thanksgiving is the trigger that prepares us for the miracle-working power of God.

Understanding Praise Words

"The best way to understand what praise means is to examine the words used for praise in the Old Testament," says Law.[9] *Hallelujah* simply means praise the Lord. It is a combination of the Hebrew words *halal* and *Jehovah*. It means to be boastful, to be excited, and to enjoy. This word connotes a tremendous explosion of enthusiasm in the act of praising. For the person wanting to be healed, simply singing, shouting, or saying "hallelujah!" has tremendous power.

Yadah is used as a public acknowledgement, as in Psalm 138:1: "I will praise Thee with my whole heart; before the gods will I sing praise unto thee." The root meaning of this word has to do with the extended hand or throwing out the hand. It implies worshiping with raised hands. The warring sick person needs to worship often with action, throwing his hands upward in power. When Jehoshaphat's choir went before the army, they lifted their hands with all their strength and said, "Praise (*yadah*) the Lord; for his mercy endureth forever (2 Chron. 20:19-21)." This is the opposite of wringing one's hands in despair when the doctor has given a bad report.

The Hebrew word *barak* simply means to bless. Terry Law says that there is a sense of kneeling and blessing God as an act of adoration in the word *barak*.[10] The word is often translated as bowing down in a worshipful attitude. When the person is sick, he should take time from all the running around and simply kneel before the Lord, staying there, blessing Him, expecting to receive the promise of His healing touch. During this kind of worship, one can expect a miracle. Note Psalm 72:15: "...let them bless (*barak*) Him all day long" (NAS).

Zamar is another word of praise. This is one of the musical verbs for *praise* in the Book of Psalms.[11] It carries with it the idea of making music in praise to God as in Psalm 92:1: "It is a good thing to give thanks unto the Lord, and to sing praises unto Thy name, O most High." Law affirms that it is impossible to understand praise without understanding its relationship to music.[12] *Zamar* means to touch the strings and refers to praise that involves instrumental worship as delineated in

Psalm 150. For one who is sick, music is very effective therapy. In his delightful book, *Praise Faith in Action*, Charles Trombley tells of a group in Long Island who held an all-night New Year's party where everyone came expecting to participate with praise and various kinds of instruments. The director had laid a $30,000 need for property before the Lord and had a praise party. The next day they received a check for $30,000 for the property. Later the director's wife was healed from advanced terminal cancer the same way—a praise party with musical instruments.[13]

Shabach is another word for praise. This word is used in Psalm 117:1: "O Praise the Lord, all ye nations: praise Him, all ye people." This word as used here means to laud, or to speak well of in a high and befitting way. It also means to address in a loud tone, to command triumph and glory, or to shout. There is a time when it is appropriate to give a loud shout unto the Lord. This is the kind of praise that makes the devil shut up. The *shabach* is effective everywhere: at church, at home, while driving. The shout will often set sick people free. Psalm 47:1 reads, "Shout unto God with the voice of triumph." It works! Every sick person should be encouraged to worship in this manner.

The next Hebrew word for praise is *towdah*. In the New American Standard Bible, it is translated as "thanksgiving." It is used in the Book of Psalms to thank God for things that have not yet happened, as well as for those things already completed. "Towdah" is directly related to the concept of sacrifice as it relates to praise.[14] If we are willing to offer up a sacrifice of praise now, then we shall see a manifestation of the salvation of God. In other words, we must praise Him before the event. The sacrifice of praise as an act of faith is implicit in the word *towdah*. It is rejoicing in something that is promised in the Word but which has not yet taken place. Terry Law says, "This is what happens in my praise and healing rallies when I encourage people to praise the Lord before there has been any manifestation of healing from God. As people raise their hearts and hands in praise to the Lord, it involves a sacrifice, especially if they are very sick in their bodies."[15]

Tehillah is another Hebrew word meaning to sing or to laud. It is the singing forth of our halals. This word is used in Psalm 22:3 where we read that God inhabits (sits enthroned on) the praises of His people. God manifests Himself in the midst of exuberant singing. In Second Chronicles 20:22, when Israel began to sing and to praise God, He set ambushments. This word refers to a special kind of singing: it is the singing of unprepared, unrehearsed songs; probably what we would know today as singing in the Spirit. Other references are Psalms 34:1, 40:3, and 66:2. In Ephesians 5:18-19, Paul tells us to "...be filled with the Spirit; speaking to yourselves in psalms and hymns and spiritual songs... " This *tehillah* singing isn't just spirit singing; however, it is songs of the Spirit, unprepared, unpremeditated, that simply flow forth as a result of being filled with the Spirit. A person desiring healing should sing this way. In private times we can begin to sing the Word or sing whatever God is saying at that particular time. It is a wonderful avenue of healing.

Another word for praise is *ruah*. This word means to shout with joy. Psalm 95:1 says, "Let us make a joyful noise to the rock of our salvation." Psalm 100:1 commands, "Make a joyful noise unto the Lord... ." Every sick person should be encouraged to shout with joy and sing joyful songs to the Lord.

Each of these words for praise are words of sound. Terry Law says, "Praise in the Old Testament always is accompanied with sound. It is vocal, it is public, and it is excited."[16] In all these ways of praise, one can use the mighty weapons of the Name, the Word, and the Blood.

Praise Prepares the Way for Miracles

Praise prepares the way for the supernatural miracle-working power of God. When the devil comes against us, praise will make a way of escape. Psalm 50:23 declares, "Whoso offereth praise glorifieth Me: and to him that ordereth his conversation aright will I shew the salvation of God." The word translated *salvation* here refers to the salvation of the body as well as the soul. It refers directly to deliverance from satanic attack. When we offer up the sacrifice of praise, God will show us His salvation by coming to us with deliverance. This means that through praise we have prepared a way for Him to intervene.

Jonah was in the belly of the fish when he talked about the water compassing him about and the weeds wrapping around his neck. But in chapter two verse 9 he said, "But I will sacrifice unto thee with the voice of thanksgiving... ." In the next verse the Bible says, "The Lord spake unto the fish and it vomited out Jonah upon the dry land." Something about his praise lined him up for deliverance. Law says, "In our prayer we must stay away from complaining and offer a sacrifice of praise. Then God speaks to the source of our complaint and brings deliverance."[17]

Praise Stops Our Enemies

Psalm 8:2 tells us, "Out of the mouth of babes and sucklings hast thou ordained strength because of thine enemies, that thou mightest still the enemy and the avenger." God has ordained praise as a weapon to stop the enemy. Since sickness is a number one enemy for many, praise can stop this enemy as it comes against the bodies of God's children.

Praising God in the Dance

Dancing before the Lord is another powerful way of worshiping God. Psalm 149:3 commands, "Let them praise His name in the dance." This kind of praise also greatly benefits the warrior. In Psalm 30:11 David testifies, "Thou hast turned for me my mourning into dancing." Robert Gay maintains, "When we dance, we put the devil under our feet."[18] When a person is physically able, he should dance before the Lord, expecting the devil to stop the fight because he is under the feet of the warrior.

The Prayer Missile

Prayer is one of the greatest missiles for launching the warheads. In John 16:24, Jesus said, "Hitherto have ye asked nothing in My name: ask, and ye shall receive... ." Jesus declares here that the prayer prayed in His name will receive His attention. This puts prayer on a legal basis, for He has given us the legal right to use His name. E.W. Kenyon says, "As we take our privilege and rights and pray in Jesus' name, it passes out of our hands into the hands of Jesus; He then assumes the responsibility of that prayer, and we know that He said, 'Father, I thank thee that thou hearest me.' In other words, we know that the Father always hears Jesus, and when we pray in Jesus' name, it is as though Jesus Himself were doing the praying. He takes our place. When we pray, we take Jesus' place here to carry out His will, and He takes our place before the Father."[19]

God Has No Favorites in Prayer

Thousands of people are depending solely on the prayers of other people as though God will hear others rather than them. To be healed, you have the right to do your own asking, your own believing, your own receiving. Go to God, quote His Word and see the healing come.

Agreement in Prayer Can Bring Healing

When a person has a prayer partner, for some reason there is much more power. Deuteronomy 32:30 and Joshua 23:10 both indicate that with God, one believer can chase a thousand enemies; yet two together can put ten thousand to flight.

Let me admonish those needing healing that in spite of the benefits of united prayer, they must learn to stand alone at times. Kenneth Hagin says, "It is easy to get healed in a mass meeting where there is a mass faith and everybody's believing...But when these people get back home on their own, they're really on their own. They're not surrounded by faith any longer. Many times they're surrounded by doubt and unbelief. Then the minute the first symptoms show up, they say, 'I thought the Lord healed me, but I guess He didn't.' And when they say that, they open the door to the devil. Instead of rising up and meeting the devil with the Word of God and commanding his power to be broken, they yield. Why? Because they have no foundation of God's word in their lives. They are depending on others to carry them on their prayers and faith...A permanent healing will be based on their own faith. No one can maintain a healing which has come as a result of another's faith, gifts of the Spirit, and so on, unless his faith is developed through the Word of God to the point where he can maintain his own rights."[20]

There are times, however, when another person in agreement brings the needed healing. John G. Lake writes of his sister's illness and healing at a point when they thought she was gone: "I discovered this strange fact, that there are times when one's spirit lays hold on the spirit of another. I just felt my spirit lay hold on the spirit of that sister. And I prayed, 'Dear Lord, she cannot go.' I walked up and down the room for some time. My spirit was crying out for somebody with faith in God that I could call upon to help me...As I walked up and down in my sister's room, I could think of but one man who had faith on this line. That was John Alexander Dowie, six hundred miles away. I went to the phone, called Western Union and told them I wanted to get a telegram through to Dr. Dowie with an answer back as quickly as possible. I sent this wire; 'My sister has apparently died, but my spirit will not let her go. I believe if you will pray, God will heal her.' I received this answer back: 'Hold on to God. I am praying. She will live.' I have asked a thousand times, 'What would it have meant if instead of that telegram of faith, I had received one from a weakling preacher who might have said, 'I am afraid you are on the wrong track,' or 'Brother, you are excited,' or 'the days of miracles are past'? It was the strength of his faith that came over the wire that caused the lightnings of my soul to begin to flash, and while I stood at the telephone and listened, the very lightnings of God began to flash in my spirit. I prayed, 'This thing is of hell; it cannot be; it will not be. In the name of Jesus Christ, I abolish this death and sickness, and she shall live.' And as I finished praying, I turned my eyes toward the bed, and saw her eyelids blink...Five days later she came to father's home and sat down with us to Christmas dinner."[21]

Healing Groups Can Bring Healing

Francis McNutt, a former Catholic priest, speaks of "soaking prayer" in his book *The Power to Heal.*[22] Mark Virkler picks up on that theme in his newsletter, in which he gives a pattern which he used in a retreat for praying for the sick in groups. Virkler says, "We did a healing prayer workshop using soaking prayer, having people break into groups and pray for about twenty minutes for the person in the center of the group. We specifically designed the groups so that the sick individual would have a unique gifting of people around them. First would be a person who was suffering from the same ailment as they. (This person would have empathy.) Another person would be one who had been healed from the same condition. (This person would have faith.) A third person would be a close friend or family member. (This person would have compassion.) Then others could join as they desired."[23]

Calling for the Elders is Calling for More Troops

In the Great Commission that Christ gave His disciples in Mark 16:17-18, He said, "And these signs shall follow them that believe; in My name shall they cast out devils…they shall lay hands on the sick, and they shall recover." James 5:14-15 states, "Is any sick among you? let him call for the elders of the church; and let them pray over him, anointing him with oil in the name of the Lord: and the prayer of faith shall save the sick, and the Lord shall raise him up." McCrossan reminds us: "The word for save here is *sosei*, the future, 3rd singular of *sozo*, the very word used by Christ every time he said to a sick person, 'Thy faith hath made thee whole.' "[24] Also read carefully the following verses: Matthew 9:22; Mark 6:56; Mark 10:52; Luke 8:48; Luke 17:19. This kind of healing is a part of God's Word. When it is obeyed, God marvelously fulfills His promise.

Diligence in Prayer is Required

Diligence is required of the one who is praying for healing. God is the rewarder of those who diligently seek Him. Thousands of people undergo major surgery and take their medicine diligently without any promise of being healed. Yet when coming to God for healing, which God positively promises to give, many do not come with that kind of diligence.

Persistence is necessary for being healed of major diseases. Some have held to the philosophy that they ask only once, fearing that to ask again would show unbelief. In most healings, however, except for instantaneous miracles, persistence is what pays off. The woman of Canaan mentioned in Matthew 15:21-28 came to Jesus to ask for the healing of her daughter. She was an alien to the commonwealth of Israel. She was a stranger to the covenant of God. She had no "right" to healing. In fact, she was a devotee of a heathen religion. Everything was against her. Even the disciples were trying to get the Lord to get rid of her. He said to her, "I am not sent but unto the lost sheep of the house of Israel." Then He said, "It is not meet to take the children's bread, and to cast it to dogs." He was obviously calling her a dog, a type of everything unclean. Yet she persisted and got her prayer answered. Jesus said to her, "O woman, great is thy faith: be it unto thee even as thou wilt." Persistence pays off.

Use the Mighty Warheads in Prayer

The warrior will be the victor if he uses the Word, the name of Jesus, and the blood of Jesus in his prayer life. These mighty warheads, launched into orbit through the prayer missile, will bring destruction to the devil's attack.

Pray the Word, not the problem. God's Word is our contact with Him. We put Him in remembrance of His Word (Is. 43:26). We remind Him that He is the Lord that healeth us. His Word does not return to Him void—without producing results—but it shall accomplish that which He pleases and purposes, and it shall prosper in the thing for which He sent it (Is. 55:11).

Use the name of Jesus, that mighty warhead, in prayer. John 14:13-15 records one of the most staggering promises and commandments ever made by Jesus: "And whatsoever ye shall ask in My name, that will I do, that the Father may be glorified in the Son. If ye shall ask anything in My name, I will do it. If ye love Me, keep My commandments." That name has been given to us for our use. When we pray in His name Scripturally, it is as though Christ Himself has prayed. There is no sickness, no demon, no person that can prevent the answer to the prayer in the name of Jesus. Use it!

While praying, picture the blood of Jesus flowing over the altar of God. That blood is just as powerful today as it has ever been. Declare the blood of Jesus in your prayer life. Because of that blood, we are clothed with righteousness. That robe is the perfect blood of Jesus. One drop of His blood is enough to heal any disease. The blood speaks! It speaks healing.

These warheads are destructive to sickness. Let the prayer missile destroy the satanic stronghold of sickness.

The Confession Missile

The sick person can war with the Word through his confession. In Hebrews 3:1, Christianity is called a profession. Bosworth says that the Greek word translated *profession* is the same as the one translated *confession*.[25] He says that the word means "to say the same thing." He goes on to explain: "It means to believe and say what God says about our sins, our sickness, and everything else included in our redemption."[26] It must be noted, however, that confessing the Word is not the same as denying one's sickness. A person cannot war for healing until he knows that his sickness is a real enemy.

Bosworth maintains, "We are commanded to consider Christ Jesus as the high priest of our confession. As our high priest, Jesus acts in our behalf according to what we confess, when it is in accord with God's word."[27]

Wrong Confession Brings the Opposite of Healing

Bosworth goes on to say, "Confessing disease is like signing for the package that the express company has delivered. Satan has a receipt from you showing that you have accepted it."[29] Peter says, "If any man speak, let him speak as the oracles of God." (1 Pet. 4:11a) Ephesians 4:29 commands us to speak only "that which is good to the use of edifying."

Speak God's Language

The sick person must say what God's Word says. He must agree with God by agreeing with His Word. He must not call things as they are; he must call them as God's Word says they should be. Confession either heals or keeps you sick. *God's* words upon your lips become as powerful as if He were saying them Himself.

"Thou shalt also decree a thing, and it shall be established unto thee" (Job 22:28). The words you speak are vital to your health and well-being. Charles Capps says, "There are some diseases that will never be cured unless people learn to speak the language of health that the body understands. God's Word is infused (engrafted) into you by giving voice to His Word with your own mouth, and this is the language of health to your body."[29]

Joel 3:10 says, "Let the weak say, I am strong." Kenyon declares, "This is the paradox of faith: to say I am strong when I am weak."[30]

Confessions That Aid the Warrior

In his delightful booklet *God's Creative Power for Healing*,[31] Charles Capps has provided some tremendous confessions which I personally used during my crisis with cancer. Some of them are as follows:

> Jesus is the Lord of my life. I forbid sin, sickness, and disease to have any power over me. I am forgiven and free from sin and guilt. I am dead to sin and alive unto the righteousness of God (Col. 1:21-22).

> Jesus bore my sickness and carried my pain. Therefore I give no place to sickness or pain. For God sent His word and healed me (Ps. 107:20).

> As God was with Moses, so is He with me. My eyes shall not be dim; neither will my natural

power be abated. Blessed are my eyes, for they see, and my ears, for they hear.

Jesus took my infirmities and bore my sicknesses. Therefore I refuse to allow sickness to dominate my body. The life of God flows in my body and brings healing to every fiber of my being (Mt. 8:17; Jn. 6:63).

Because I am redeemed from the curse, I declare that the truth of Galatians 3:13 is flowing in my bloodstream. It flows to every cell of my body, restoring health and life (Mk. 11:23; Lk. 17:6).

Father, your life is in me. First Peter 2:24 flows in my bloodstream, restoring every cell of my body. Your word is made a reality in my flesh, and life is restored to every cell of my body in Jesus' name.

That which God has not planted is dissolved and rooted out of this body in Jesus' name. First Peter 2:24 is engrafted into every fiber of my being, and my body is alive with the life of God (Mk. 11:23; Jn. 6:63).

I am redeemed from the curse, and I forbid growths and tumors to inhabit my body. The life of God in my blood dissolves growths and tumors, and my strength and health is restored (Mt. 16:19; Jn. 14:13, Mk. 11:23).

Every organ and tissue of my body functions in the perfection to which God created it to function.

I forbid any malfunction in my body in Jesus' name (Gen. 1:28,31).

Father, your word has become a part of me. It is flowing in my blood stream. It flows to every cell of my body, restoring and transforming my body. Your word is becoming flesh; for you sent your word and healed me (Jas. 1:21; Ps. 107:20; Prov. 13:3).

Thank you, Father, that I have a strong heart. My heart beats with the rhythm of life. My blood flows to every cell of my body restoring life and health abundantly (Prov. 12:14; 14:30).

My blood pressure is 120 over 80. The life of God flows in my blood and cleanses my arteries of all matter that does not pertain to life.

I have a strong heart. Every heartbeat sends the life of God flowing through my veins, cleansing my body of sickness and disease. My blood is pure, and it destroys every disease germ and every virus that attacks my body (Eph. 3:19-20; Ex. 23-25; Mk. 11:23).

I speak to my blood. I command every red and white cell to destroy every disease germ, virus or alien cell that tries to inhabit my body. In Jesus' name I command every cell of my body to be normal. I forbid any malfunction in my body cells (Rom. 5:17; Lk. 17:6).

My immune system grows stronger day by day. I speak life to my immune system. I forbid confusion in my immune system. The same spirit that raised Christ from the dead dwells in me and quickens my immune system with the life of God, and it guards the life and health of my body.

Here is another confession that I picked up at Rhema Bible College's School of Healing:[32]

According to Proverbs 17:22, "A merry heart doeth good like a medicine: but a broken spirit drieth the bones." Ha, ha, ha, ha, ha, ha, ha! I have a merry heart. Sickness can't dominate me. Satan can't dominate me. What do you think you're trying to do, devil? You can't put sickness on me. Ha, ha, ha, ha, ha, ha, ha, ha, ha, ha, ha! I have a merry heart. I'm full of joy. A merry heart works like a medicine. God's medicine is working in me!

The Resistance Missile

Another missile with which the sick person wars is resistance. The Bible says that we must not "give place to the devil" (Eph. 4:27). James exhorts, "Resist the devil, and he will flee from you" (Jas. 4:7). Too often Christians pet and indulge their aches and pains instead of resisting them as the work of the devil. Disease must be treated as something from hell and not pampered.

Resist With the Word

"It is written" is one of the strongest ways of resisting. Bosworth says, "All the devil heard from the lips of

Christ, when tempting Him was, 'It is written. It is written' (Mt. 4:4,7,10). 'Then the devil leaveth him' (Mt. 4:11). But all we hear from people is 'The devil said,' as though Christ's works were of less consequence than those of the devil."[33] When the devil hears the Word of God, his power dissolves.

Resist With Loud Words

According to Norvel Hayes, sometimes the best way to resist is by shouting out, "No, you don't. No you don't!"[34] A sick person should loudly tell the devil what he is to do. Some say we should not give the devil any credit. They feel he should be ignored. But nowhere does the Bible tell us to ignore the devil. It tells us to resist him.

Barbara Yee of Detroit, Michigan, was told that she had cancer. She immediately started pacing the floor. She shouted, "Devil, you dropped your package off at the wrong door. Get it and take it somewhere else, because I don't want it." She was healed.

Smith Wigglesworth tells about the night before the great healing of a man named Lazarus. He said, "When I got to bed it seemed as if the devil tried to place on me everything that he had placed on that poor man in the bed. When I awoke I had a cough and all the weakness of a tubercular patient. I rolled out of bed on the floor and cried out to God to deliver me from the power of the devil. I shouted loud enough to wake everybody in the house."[35]

Speak to Symptoms When They Return

When symptoms reoccur after healing has taken place, it is necessary to speak to them like this: "Cancer, you cannot live in my body. I told you you could not stay. Now get out, in Jesus' name."

The Preaching Missile

Preaching is another powerful missile. Terry Law says, "Preaching carries the Word, the Name, and the Blood into the hearts of God's people and into the hearts of the unsaved."[36]

Preaching Brings Healing to the Preacher

When a minister gets sick, he should keep preaching the healing message. Every time he stands up to preach the Word of God, he declares to the strongholds in his life that he has authority over them.

Immediately after fighting for my life against cancer, I went to downtown Detroit and rented a building to conduct a healing school. The people who came were healed, but the biggest blessing was to my own faith.

Preaching brings healing to others

Fuchsia Pickett was a Methodist preacher who did not believe in divine healing. There had been six deaths in her family, including her father and two brothers, and she had to be carried from a hospital to her father's funeral. Nurses had packed her carefully onto a stretcher so that her backbone would not vibrate, causing it to break in pieces. After the funeral, while leaving in an ambulance, she waved back at her father's casket and said, "I will join you, Daddy, in a few months."

A few months earlier, her sick father had walked into her room and said, "Pastor, I think we have missed something. I think we have missed knowing the God of Elijah." Fuchsia had said, "Daddy, we don't need that now. Healing is not for us today. That which is perfect has come."

A few months after her father's death, she slipped into a small church to visit, thinking it would be the last one she would ever attend. A seventy-year-old man was preaching. God had awakened him at four o'clock in the morning and instructed him to preach on "Where is the Lord God of Elijah?" He had obeyed. As he preached, he declared, "If you had the faith of Elijah, you could see what Elijah saw." Then he stepped from behind the pulpit and said to Fuchsia, "My beloved, you may have followed the dearest one on earth to you and left him on a green mound, but He wants you to know that He did not take his God away from you. The God of Elijah is in this church today."

Fuchsia ordered her friend to stand her up. She went to the front for prayer. After prayer she returned to her seat. When she reached the seventh row, she heard the voice of God say, "If ye be willing and obedient, ye shall eat the good of the land." Standing there in her braces, she knew she was going to live. She stood to testify. She later said, "The power of God struck the base of my cranium. It traveled down my spine and came back up to my head. One hour and twenty minutes later, I had danced all over that church, right out of my braces."[37]

The Binding, Loosing, and Rooting Up Missile

Binding and loosing is important in the healing process of the warring sick Christian. Jesus said, "Whatsoever ye shall bind on earth shall be bound in heaven; and whatsoever ye shall loose on earth shall be loosed in heaven" (Mt. 18:18). The sick person must bind the spirit of infirmity, then loose the healing power in his life.

In the authority of Jesus name we can root up sickness, disease, and infirmity. Matthew 15:13, "Every plant, which my heavenly Father hath not planted, shall be rooted up" is the verse that became a "rhema" to me in my time of crisis with cancer.

Marilyn Hickey, in her excellent book *Be Healed*, tells a moving story about a woman who decided to root out cancer for another person. Marilyn writes, "The doctor stood at the woman's bedside shaking his head in unbelief...There was no cancer in the woman's body. Two weeks ago the patient had been given only twenty-four hours to live...One individual had believed in God's marvelous power to heal. This person had never met the dying woman but she had heard of the woman's plight through a friend. Fierce anger and intense hope had risen up inside her like a geyser—anger at the devil's disease and hope in God's ability to heal...The woman prayed, 'You foul spirit of cancer, leave this woman's body. I curse you in Jesus' name, and I command this cancer to die at the roots. It shall find no place in this body to stay.' Within the critical 24 hours, the woman reported that she could feel something moving in her body...In a day or two the patient, who was still alive, began to vomit large quantities of some odd substance. When the vomiting ceased, the woman began a remarkable recovery. All the doctors could say when the lab test came back clear was, 'She vomited the cancer from her body.' "[38] The intercessor had rooted out the cancer.

The Generational Curse-Breaking Missile

One of the ways in which we can be attacked by sickness, disease, and infirmity is through the door of inheritance. If one family member has had a particular disease, others in the family may be attacked by the same affliction. The enemy comes in any door that he can possibly open to kill and to destroy.

But this, too, can be rooted up. Marilyn Hickey says, "We can lay the ax of God's Word to the root of that tree, free ourselves from any generational curse,' and stop it from bearing bad fruit in future generations."[39] Isaiah says, "And they that shall be of thee shall build the old waste places: thou shalt raise up the foundations of many generations; and thou shalt be called, The repairer of the breach, The restorer of paths to dwell in" (Is. 58:12). If heart trouble runs in a person's family, he can take hold of the Word of God, the Name of Jesus, and the Blood of Jesus, and can come against satan and that evil inheritance. This works with any generational curse.

The Testimony Missile

The world is waiting for someone who will tell of his personal healing experience as well as tell how the Word of God worked in his time of crisis. When a person has a serious illness, he wants someone who has traveled that same road and emerged victorious. Terry Law explains, "If someone says God doesn't heal today, and you testify to the fact that He healed you of this disease or that disease, that settles the argument. Everyone will listen to a personal testimony."[40] Some of the great men of God share often of their notable healings. Some examples are Oral Roberts and Kenneth Hagin. Roberts tells of his collapsing on a gymnasium floor playing basketball at seventeen years of age. He tells how his sister said, "Oral, you are going to be healed." Hagin tells the story of being bedfast at sixteen years of age and God miraculously healing him. These giants in the healing ministry testify of their personal healings because they know the powerful impact their testimony can have on others. Terry Law again explains, "When we launch our testimony, we unleash a spiritual law and that law is just as true and unbreakable as the laws of physics."[41]

The Grace Missile

I have been asked many times about the person with physical handicaps. On one occasion I had spoken on spiritual warfare and healing at a retreat in Kentucky. The young lady who sang immediately before I ministered had a deformed body. Her spirit, however, was electrifying. When she sang, she brought the very presence of God into the meeting. She prepared the atmosphere for me to minister healing to other people. When I returned home and was telling about her dynamic ministry, someone asked me a puzzling question: "Was she healed?" Many times we simply do not have all the answers. On many such occasions God's grace goes into operation and a person with handicaps does not have to be stopped. They, too, can win and be greatly used of God in spite of their handicap. There are examples today of people who have refused to be stopped and overcome by handicaps. They have tapped onto powerful sources of strength, courage, and power. Someone has said, "There is only one insurmountable handicap and that is the loss of inner power. Nothing else is unconquerable. It is what is in your brain that counts."

Many of the greatest people in history have had tremendous handicaps. John Milton was blind; yet he wrote *Paradise Lost* and *Paradise Regained.* Fanny Crosby was also blind; yet she left us over 9,000 hymns when she died. Louis Braille and many others were blind, but their handicap did not stop them. Lord Byron was crippled. So was Franklin D. Roosevelt. Thomas Edison was nearly deaf. Ludwig van Beethoven, one of the world's greatest composers, lost his hearing completely; yet he completed his famous Ninth Symphony. Helen Keller was blind, deaf, and until later in her life, mute.

Carol Schuller, the daughter of Robert Schuller, is a striking example of someone who has allowed God's grace to make her an overcomer. The Schullers were in Korea when Carol had a motorcycle accident. She was in critical condition, losing seventeen pints of blood. When they got her to the hospital, she had no pulse. In spite of her condition her life was spared, though one of her legs had to be amputated below the knee. Schuller writes of that time: "I remember those trying months of 1978 when Mrs. Schuller and I were spending many hours with our daughter Carol who had had her leg amputated below the knee. We struggled with uncertainty, not knowing whether or not the doctors would be able to save her knee or her thigh. And I remember how much comfort we received when Carol looked at us and said, 'I'll tell you one thing, Dad, if they take my knee and if they take my thigh, it won't change God's plan for my life one bit!' "[42] He continues, "God's plan doesn't rest on whether you have an eye, or whether you can speak or hear."[43]

Shortly after her recuperation, Carol spent her Thanksgiving holiday learning to ski. Flying from Los Angeles to Denver, she took skiing instructions from Hal O'-Leary, whom Schuller says has trained over one thousand amputees to ski. He further writes, "By the third day she was gliding gracefully down the longest slopes, jumping moguls—doing fabulously."[44]

When Carol was seventeen, the Schullers were on a boat cruise in the Hawaiian Islands with the American-Hawaiian Steamship Company. It was customary on the last night of this cruise to have a talent show in which the passengers participated. Carol decided to enter the contest. The Schullers wondered what she would do since she did not sing. Many of the passengers participated in the contest, but when Carol came on the platform, Schuller says, "She came on stage wearing neither shorts nor Hawaiian garb, but a full-length dress. She looked beautiful. She walked up to the microphone and said, 'I really don't know what my talent is, but I thought this would be a good chance for me to do what I think I owe you all, and that is an explanation. I know you've been looking at me all week, wondering about my fake leg. I thought I should tell you what happened. I was in a motorcycle accident. I almost died, but they kept giving me blood, and my pulse came back. They amputated my leg below the knee and later they amputated through the knee. I spent seven months in the hospital, seven months with intravenous antibiotics to fight infection...If I've but one talent, it is this: I can tell you that during that time my faith became very real to me...I look at you girls and you walk without a limp. I wish I could walk that way. I can't, but this is what I've learned, and I want to leave it with you—it's not how you walk that counts, but Who walks with you and Who you walk with. Jesus walks with me, and I walk with Him, and I'm happy. Thank you."[45] Schuller stated that there was not a person there who was not touched that night.

David Ring is a man who minsters to thousands that God's grace is sufficient. When he was born in 1953, there was no oxygen to his brain for eighteen minutes. He was a cripple with cerebral palsy. His parents were good to him and loved him and made him happy by convincing him that he was special. At the age of eleven, David's life took another turn when his father died. When he was fourteen, his mother died. He became lonely and wanted to die. Members of his family finally gave up on him. They thought he would never do anything or be anything. He did not want to go to school and be laughed at because his body was different. He began to question whether God really loved him. Why was he born like this, he wondered? Why dia God take his mother and father? He did not want to go to church, but his one sister kept on encouraging him to go. Finally one night he went just to get her "off his back." But God spoke to him in that service about a relationship with Him. David cried out, "God, I'm a nobody; but I want to be a somebody." Then in 1971 God called him to preach the gospel. He argued, "I can't preach. I have cerebral palsy. I talk funny." But God called him anyway, even though he can't even say Jesus plainly. On one occasion in a service aired on Jerry Falwell's Old Time Gospel Hour TV program, David testified, "They said, 'Nobody will have you in their church.' But I spoke 263 times in the last twelve months...They said, 'You will never find a wife. No woman wants to live with you,' but in 1981 God and me showed them...The told me I would never be a daddy... but I am four times." He closed his message with the challenge: "I have cerebral palsy. What's your problem?"

Joni Eareckson is an unforgettable young woman who also shows us how to be an overcomer. As a young girl Joni had dived into what she did not know was shallow water in the Chesapeake Bay, and as a result she has had to struggle against quadriplegia and depression. After surgery the reality hit that she would never walk again. Then the news came that she would not ever regain the use of her arms and hands. But she did allow God's grace to work in her. She returned to her artwork. Though she used a pen or a brush in her mouth, her art took on a new quality and professionalism. She experimented with different pens and brushes, finally settling on a sharp, felt-tip flair pen. She signs her drawings PTL (Praise the Lord). She says, "God has ingrained the reflection of Christ into my character, developed my happiness, my patience, my purpose in life. He has given me contentment. My art is a reflection of how God can empower someone like me to rise above circumstances."[46] Today Joni's art has gone around the world and she speaks to thousands.

When the devil gives you a lemon, you let God make lemonade. The problem too often is that we don't want to give God the lemons. Someone has said, "Whatever stick the devil has beaten you with, take it and beat him back with it." For one who has gone through a crisis that has left him "not normal," spiritual warfare is the answer. The fight may be tough, but the impact of that warrior's life will be great. Only eternity will reveal all of the blessings that will come to people around the world through such a warrior who will not be stopped by his handicap.

The Launching of all Weapons with the Human Mouth

"Every one of the weapons is launched with the human mouth," declares Terry Law.[47] We praise and worship with our mouths. We pray with our mouths. We confess with our mouths. We preach with our mouths. We resist with our mouths. We bind and loose with our mouths. Law further states, "With our mouths, we can launch God's rockets or the devil's rockets. It is up to us to make the choice."[48] In fact, you, yourself, can become the missile that God will use to bring healing to others. Just open your mouth!

Warfare Healing Principles

- The warring missles carry the warheads to the place for destruction of the enemy.

- We enter into the power and presence of the Lord through praise and worship.

- Praise prepares the way for the supernatural miracle-working power of God.

- Praise stops the enemy.

- One may not be able to maintain a healing which has come as a result of another's faith.

- Pray the Word, not the problem.

- Say what God says and shut up.

- Wrong confession brings the opposite of healing.

- Speak God's language.

- The resistance missile is like dynamite.

- Disease must be treated as something from hell and must not be pampered.

- Resist with the Word.

- Resist with loud words.

- Speak to symptoms.

- Preaching carries the warheads into the hearts of people.

- Binding puts chains on the enemy and takes the key out of the door.

- Bind sickness and loose health.

- Lay the ax of God's Word to the root of the generational curse tree.

- Everyone will listen to a personal testimony.

- Many of the greatest people in history have had great handicaps.

- When the devil gives you a lemon, let God make lemonade. The problem too often is that we don't want to give God the lemons.

- Every one of the rockets is launched with the human mouth.

Endnotes

1. Norvel Hayes, *How to Live and Not Die* (Tulsa, OK: Harrison House, 1986), p. 15.

2. Marilyn Hickey, *Be Healed* (Denver, CO: Marilyn Hickey Ministries, 1992), p. 95.

3. Norvel Hayes, op. cit., p. 11.

4. Ibid., p. 12.

5. Don Gossett, *Praise Avenue*, Copyright 1976, used by permission of the Publisher, Whitaker House, 580 Pittsburgh Street, Springdale, PA, 15144, pp. 69-71.

6. Norvel Hayes, *How to Live and Not Die*, pp. 16-17.

7. Terry Law, *The Power of Praise and Worship*, p. 117.

8. Ibid, p. 119.

9. Ibid, p. 130.

10. Ibid., p. 131.

11. Ibid., p. 132.

12. Ibid.

13. Charles Trombley, *Praise Faith in Action* (Indianola, IA: Fountain Press, 1978), pp. 32-33.

14. Law, op. cit., pp. 133-134.

15. Ibid, p. 134.

16. Ibid, p. 135.

17. Ibid, p. 155.

18. Message by Robert Gay at Santa Rosa Beach, FL, September, 1992.

19. Kenyon, *The Wonderful Name of Jesus*, p. 4.

20. Kenneth Hagin, *How to Keep Your Healing*, (Tulsa, OK: Hagin Ministries, 1987), pp. 13-14.

21. Gordan Lindsay, *John G. Lake, Apostle to Africa* (Dallas; Christ for the Nations, 1972), pp. 12-13. Nations, 1972.

22. Francis McNutt, *The Power to Heal* (New York: Bantam Books, 1980), pp. 20-50.

23. Mark Virkler, "Prayer and Fasting Retreat,"*Communion with God*, September 1992, p. 16.

24. McCrossan, p. 42.

25. F.F. Bosworth, *Christ the Healer* (New York: Fleming H. Revell, a division of Baker Book House Co., 1877), p. 139.

26. Ibid.

27. Bosworth, p. 138.

28. Ibid., p. 142.

29. Charles Capps, *God's Creative Power for Healing* (Tulsa, OK: Harrison House, Inc., 1991), p. 7.

30. E.W. Kenyon and Don Gossett, *The Power of the Positive Confession* (Lynnwood, WA: Kenyon Gospel Publishing Co., 1977), p. 92.

31. Capps, Ibid., pp. 24-34.

32. Handout received at Rhema Bible College, May, 1990.

33. Bosworth, p. 102.

34. Norvel Hayes, *How to Live and Not Die*, Tape 1.

35. Smith Wigglesworth, *Ever Increasing Faith*, p. 31.

36. Law, p. 113.

37. Fuchsia Pickett, *God's Dream* (Shippensburg, PA: Destiny Image, 1991), pp. 44-49.

38. Marilyn Hickey, pp. 147-148.

39. Ibid., p. 25.

40. Law, p. 116.

41. Ibid., p. 117.

42. Robert Schuller, *Trust for the Crust,* (Hour of Power: Orange, CA, 1979), p. 4.

43. Ibid.

44. Robert Schuller, *Test and Be Blest*, (Hour of Power, 1979), p. 6.

45. Robert Schuller, *Become a Possibility Thinker*, (Hour of Power, 1982), pp. 10-11.

46. Taken from the book, JONI by Joni Eareckson. Copyright © 1976 by Joni Eareckson and Joe Musser. Used by permission of Zondervan Publishing House.

47. Law, p. 105.

48. Ibid., p. 105.

Chapter Five

The Prophetic Word Missile

Personal prophecy is one of the greatest missiles in the arsenal of the spiritual warrior. Because of its uniqueness, I have devoted an entire chapter to our examination of it.

Not a Revealer of God's Willingness to Heal

Personal prophecy is not designed to reveal whether God is able or willing to heal. That has already been revealed by the Logos, the written Word of God. I believe I have already demonstrated beyond any doubt that the Word has promised healing to all of God's children.

When God Keeps Giving Future Direction

There are times when a prophet, not aware of a person's disease, will give a word concerning what the person will be doing in the future. When this occurs, the person can be assured that God is not yet finished with him. There are many examples of people who have received prophetic words even though they had contracted some incurable disease. As a result, their healing came.

On one occasion, Barbara Yoder was prophesying to a lady telling her what beautiful things God had planned for her life. The lady looked up and asked, "What about my cancer?" Barbara's reaction was, "You must be going to live because you will have to live for all of this to come about. Go believing that you are healed." At the time of this writing, this woman is alive and well.[1]

I had been given numerous personal prophecies concerning God using me in a healing ministry. Then came the vicious attack of breast cancer. Though the enemy tried to kill me, it was evident that God had a plan for my life. I warred with the prophetic words that had been given to me. I reminded God, "God, Your prophets have spoken that I would have a healing ministry. Scott Webster, Your prophet, said this previous April before cancer struck in July that You were going to cause miracles to take place in my ministry. You said through Your prophet that You wanted me to march back like Elisha and smite the river and walk through on dry ground. You said You would send signs and wonders to convince the gainsayers."

Warring With the Words of Seasoned Prophets

God will often give a sick person a prophetic word for encouragement, edification, and comfort. The person can then take the prophetic words of the mature, proven prophets and war with them. In *Prophets and Personal Prophecy*, Bishop Bill Hamon suggests, "Leave the 'Thus saith the Lord' to the mature, proven prophets. They are the ones who are anointed to speak a creative word of healing and miraculous deliverance."[2] He suggests that others should preface their words with, "My strong conviction is...I believe that...I am convinced that you will...The Bible declares that..."[3]

I warred with the prophetic words that came after the attack of cancer. My friend Barbara Yoder was very cautious about prophesying over me during my crisis because she did not want to prophesy solely out of her desire to see me well again. However, two weeks after I was dismissed from the hospital, she was so greatly anointed in one of our women's meetings in Detroit that she simply had to prophesy. She declared:

For the Lord would say unto you, Peggy, This night is the beginning of a new day. Have not I said to you that you would lay hands on the sick and they would recover. For I would say unto you that I will loose from you a new healing flow and there shall be signs and wonders worked by your hands in the name of Jesus of Nazareth. You shall lay hands on the sick and they shall recover. You shall not go in and look at the faces of people. But you shall go into the meetings and look at the face of the Lord your God...And you shall lay hands on them and they shall be healed. For the Lord would say unto thee, Hath not satan touched you? Did he not try to kill you? But I would not let him have you, and I am doing a new thing. This night I release in you a new anointing. I release in you an anointing for healing. For I would say unto you to begin to lay hands on them. Begin to work the workings of miracles and your hands shall cast out devils, for I have put the power in your hands...I will take you where I said I will, for I am the Lord your God.

A while later another prophetic word came. On August 28 I had discovered a new lump in the same breast from which I had previously on July 18 had a lump removed. I was sent back to Ann Arbor for another X-ray. As a friend and I sat in a restaurant on the way home, a Black man that I had never seen before interrupted us and said, "Excuse me, lady. I do not know you, but the Holy Ghost just told me that God had a special blessing for you today and that you are all right." This provided me with another message with which to war. Because of the stress of the time, I did not keep a record of this prophet's name. I do know that he was from Flint, Michigan.

In September, an intercessor I had never known or heard of sent me a letter. It said, "Peggy, Dr. Frank Tunstall, my pastor, requested prayer for you on Sunday. While another intercessor and I were praying for you, the Lord gave me Isaiah 54:14-17 for you. The impression I had while praying was that satan and his agents were making lots of noise, but that it was just noise and would dissipate as you and intercessors come against it." I warred with those words too.

In October, 1990, I attended a minister's meeting in Detroit where Bishop Bill Hamon and Scott Webster were ministering. Scott prophesied:

Daughter of mine, I have called you to move in signs and wonders and miracles and healings. The enemy saw that seed and he began to attack you in your physical body. The Lord says I am arising against that spirit of infirmity which has come against you, and I am causing your innermost being and your organs to be healed. I am causing strength to arise; and God says, Daughter of Mine, you are going to preach healing, speak healing, minister healing and miracles, and you are going to live and not die...You are going to lay hands on the sick and minister the life of God; and the power of God and healing and miracles shall be manifested says the Lord your God.

Then Bishop Hamon prayed:

Father, we agree together as a body. We curse this foul thing that has been sent by the angel of death to try to destroy this body. We destroy this assignment of hell. We rebuke you now. We curse you now. Get out of this body. We declare life and health. And your assignment is cancelled and this body will live and not die but live in victory and power from on high. In Jesus' name, we activate the healing and health of God to resist and overcome every invasion of hell.

There were other prophetic words that kept coming. My husband and I were waiting in an airport in Dallas, Texas, when we ran across Harold Woodson, an evangelist who had been in our church several years previously. After he sat down on the plane, the Lord gave him these words: "The enemy has used his finest weapon, but it will not accomplish its purpose." In addition, my sister-in-law in Greenville, South Carolina, received a strong prophetic word that the devil had sent cancer, but that it was to be turned into a ministry for healing.

For months I warred with the prophetic words of Scott Webster, the evangelist, the intercessor, my sister-in-law, Barbara Yoder, the Black man in the restaurant, and numerous others. Their words were lifesavers when fears were sent from hell to make me afraid.

Those Who See Only the Battle

There are some areas that need to be guarded. Sometimes unseasoned prophets may see only the battle and not the victory. An example is when intercessors see a person dead. They may actually see this, but God may be showing them the devil's plan so that they can break that power in prayer. Often it takes a seasoned prophet to come along and break the power of death that the devil has planned. An example of this is in the life of a dear friend of mine, a lady who is greatly used of God in the Detroit area. Her husband was the owner of a company which had experienced great difficulties in 1991. During this crisis time in the business, this lady was attacked with multiple sclerosis. During a one week period, three intercessors had come to her and said, "We have seen you dead while we were praying." But then one Saturday morning Barbara Yoder spoke in a meeting this lady was attending. Though Barbara did not know the family or the lady, she turned to my friend on the platform and said, "Come here. Let me lay my hands on you. Your business is going to be blessed. And you are going to live and not die." This broke the spirit of death that had tried to attach itself to my friend. The intercessors probably had seen her dead, but they only saw the demonic attack that was raging in the spirit world. This could have brought on premature death had not a seasoned prophetess heard the Word of the Lord.

Reversing Some Prophetic Words

It should be noted that the prophetic word may be reversed at times. An example is Hezekiah. In Isaiah 38 we read that he was "sick unto death." Isaiah the prophet came to him and said, "Thus saith the Lord, set thine house in order: for thou shalt die, and not live."

His case was now hopeless. God had pronounced death upon him. Yet he did not die. He did not even set his house in order. He turned his face to the wall and sought God. God then reversed the prophetic word. He sent Isaiah back to Hezekiah with the news that He was extending his life.

If someone should give a sick person a bad word, he should do as Hezekiah and turn his face to the wall—away from negative people, away from the one who gave the bad word. When a person turns to God, he always finds compassion.

Prophetic Words Concerning Future Healings

Sometimes a prophetic word may come to a person about a healing that will take place in the future. A striking example of this was when Leon Walters was ministering to Don Kingsmore from North Carolina in a prophetic presbytery. Leon had prophesied beautiful things that God was going to do in Don's life and business. Then, in the middle of it all, Leon began to pray prophetically. He prayed for Don's back, his neck, and the blood circulation to the brain. Afterwards Leon asked Don if he had problems with any of those areas or even headaches. Don replied, "No, I do not have headaches or any of those problems, but I receive the prophecy and the prophetic prayer anyway." A few weeks later he had a motorcycle accident and broke his neck. His wife was rushing to the intensive care unit at the hospital when she stopped by the mail box and found a tape of the prophetic presbytery from Christian International. She listened carefully to see if there was any hint of this accident in any of the prophetic words. There was nothing negative. But when she heard Leon praying prophetically for her husband, she understood that this was the time for which God had given the prophecy. She received that prayer and took it to her husband. They warred with the prophetic words. In just a few weeks Don was out of the hospital, out of all braces, completely healed. He is still healed at the time of this writing with no problems. One of the greatest miracles was that the blood never stopped flowing to the brain even though his neck had been broken.[4]

Hearing the Voice of God for Oneself

A prophetic gifting may be in development as a warrior is seeing himself well, saturating himself with the Word of God, calling those things that be not as though they were, etc. Therefore, the warrior may need to do his own prophesying. When Ezekiel went to the valley of dry bones, God told him to prophesy to the bones. Sometimes, it becomes necessary for the warrior to prophesy to his own pitiful situation.

Get Into a Quiet Place

One of the first things a person must do in order to hear the voice of God for himself is to get into a quiet place. Habakkuk said, "I will stand upon my watch, and set me upon the tower" (Hab. 2:1). Habakkuk knew that in order to hear the voice of God, he must get alone in a quiet place. In his book, *Communion with God,* [5] Mark Virkler maintains:

> In order for us to hear the still, small voice of God within us, we ourselves must become quiet. Life is such a rush. We just rush up to God, blurt out our prayers and rush away again. I am convinced we will never enter the realm of the Spirit this way...We must learn to quiet our own inner being, all the voices and thoughts calling for attention. Until they are quieted, we will most likely not hear His voice. Becoming still cannot be hurried or forced. Rather, it must be allowed to happen. At a point in your stillness, God takes over and you sense His active flow within you. His spontaneous images begin flowing with a life of their own. His voice begins flowing, giving you wisdom and strength. You find that you are in the Spirit (Rev. 1:10).

Journaling Helps Us Hear the Voice of God More Clearly

Journaling is a biblical method that can be used to help the warring person grow in discernment of the voice of God. Psalms is an example of journaling, which simply means keeping a notebook of prayers and what you sense to be God's answers. Virkler feels:

> God is speaking to His children much of the time. However, we often do not differentiate His voice

from our own thoughts, and therefore, we are timid about stepping out in faith. If we can learn to clearly discern His voice speaking within us, we will be much more confident...One of the greatest benefits of using a journal during your communion with the Lord is that it allows you to receive freely the spontaneous flow of ideas that come to your mind, in faith believing that they are from Jesus, without short-circuiting them by subjecting them to rational and sensory doubt. You can write in faith believing they are from the Lord, knowing that you will be able to test them later.[6]

During my battle with cancer, I dialogued with God in my journal. Today I treasure those prophetic words. Once, when questioning the Lord concerning my healing, I wrote what I felt was God speaking back to me:[7]

Does not my Word say you are healed? Hath not My prophets proclaimed that you would live? Arise and take My healing message to the world. Fear not, for I am with you. Do not be afraid, for I am your God. Do not look at those who have died, but look at My word that says you shall live and not die. Listen to My prophets. Concentrate on healing on the radio and in your speaking engagements. Walk close to Me and I will show you signs and wonders and miracles. Relax and watch Me work. I want you to be a vessel of honor. Be available.

Even today when I read these words, I am touched by the Holy Spirit.

Watch for Demonic Fear When Journaling About Dying

There are precautions to take in journaling when one is sick. If a person begins to journal about dying, he needs to look to God to see if this may be coming from a spirit of fear that has gripped him. When a person battling sickness gets quiet and asks God about healing, he will only get that which is biblical, for it is the will of God to bring health to His people.

Those Who Are Not Healed

The question is often asked, "Why do some people receive a word that they are healed and then they die?" Much thought has gone into this extremely difficult issue during the writing of this book. I have come to the conclusion that there are other factors that must be considered. The prophet may indeed have been right on, but the same circumstances exist that are there when the prayer of faith is prayed for a sick person. Every sick person still must war himself. He still must get the Word solidly into his spirit and war with it. It is a mystery, but healing is an individual matter. Others can pray, preach, or even prophesy, but the person must also war. There are some who do not receive their healing because they begin listening to negative people, in spite of what the Word and the prophets have said. Some just decide they want to go on to Heaven. For some, I can offer no explanation. But the Word of God is still true. Healing is still God's provision for His people. Jesus Christ is still the same yesterday, today, and forever.

War With the Words of Mature Prophets and Hear God for Yourself

We have seen that a person can war with the prophetic words of the seasoned prophets, and can also war with his own prophetic words that he gets in his quiet time with the Lord and in his journaling. Words of prophecy can be powerful and extremely helpful to those who are warring for their healing.

Warfare Healing Principles

- Personal prophecy is one of the major missiles with which we war.

- Personal prophecy does not reveal whether God is able or willing to heal. That has already been revealed by the Logos, the written Word of God.

- Take the prophetic words of the mature, proven prophets and war with them.

- A prophetic Word can be reversed at times.

- One can hear the voice of God for himself.

- Journaling helps one hear the voice of God more clearly.

Endnotes

1. Personal interview with Barbara Yoder, June, 1990.

2. Dr. Bill Hamon, *Prophets and Personal Prophecy* (Shippensburg, PA: Destiny Image, 1987), p. 41.

3. Ibid.

4. Interview with Leon Walters, March 4, 1993.

5. Mark Virkler, *Communion with God* (New York: Buffalo School of the Bible, 1983), p. 20.

6. Mark Virkler, *Communion with God*, p. 29.

7. From my personal journal.

Part Three

Victories in Battle

Chapter Six

Victories in Battle

For several years God had been leading me to teach healing on my radio program. I had started a healing school in our local church in Troy, Michigan, every Thursday morning, and people were being healed and being helped. Furthermore, prophetic words had been coming that I would have a powerful healing ministry.

Barbara Yoder, my close friend from Ann Arbor, had prophesied on February 5, 1990: "I thank you, Lord, that your gifts and callings are coming to the surface. You are putting a new word in her mouth. The word will burn like fire in her bones, a word of freedom, deliverance, and healing. She will stand before the people and the fire of God will come upon her. The people will see her change from one person to another as the mantle drops upon her."

On April 5, 1990 Scott Webster had prophesied: "Daughter of Mine, I have called you to be the prophetess of the Lord and you are going to rise and prophesy. You have been around a valley of dry bones. You have said, 'Can these bones live,' but daughter of Mine, begin to prophesy to that valley. I am going to cause miracles to take place. Deep calls unto deep...A double portion is going to be loosed on you. I want you to march back like Elisha and smite that river and walk through on dry ground. Daughter of Mine, religious folks will say, 'Where did you come from? How do you know you have Elijah's mantle?' I will send signs and wonders to convince the gainsayers... ."

God had been moving by His Spirit. Then it was as if all hell assailed me. Even though I knew a lump was there, I wasn't afraid because cancer did not run in my family. Also, I had been told that the lump was a muscle and there was nothing to fear. The gynecologist had checked me carefully in May, just one month before. It was now June 22. Besides, the mammogram a year ago had been negative. However, there was that extra heaviness that was in my heart and mind. I recalled the gynecologist saying in May, "I find no lumps, but a woman your age should have a yearly mammogram anyway."

A week later I had not heard from the doctor, so I called his office. The secretary snapped, "If there were a problem, Mrs. Scarborough, the doctor would have called you. He is a busy man." I insisted that she check my file, but she could not find my report. In just a few minutes the doctor called me back and said, "Nothing to your report. It says, 'slight thickening in left breast. X-ray again in six months.' There is no calcification and it looks good to me. However, if you would feel better, you can go to a surgeon friend of mine in Pontiac for a second opinion. I usually do not send my patients for a second opinion with a report like this, but if you were my wife, I might consider sending you. Do what you wish." I decided to have a second opinion and called immediately for an appointment.

It was July 5, 1990. I taught my healing school that morning until noon. Then my husband and I rushed to the doctor's office in Pontiac. The doctor looked at my mammogram and said, "There is no problem whatsoever." Then he checked the breast. I watched a puzzled look on his face as he said, "Don't get your hopes built up about a thing in this world. You have cancer." Out of my spirit rose the words, "I will not have cancer!" "I hope you are right," he replied. Then he did a needle biopsy and sent it along with me to the hospital.

Later, after arriving back at our church office, I immediately called the doctor to get the report from the needle biopsy. "Yes, it's cancer all right," he told me over the phone. I handed the phone to my husband and rushed off to talk to the Lord. The doctor shared with my husband my alternatives and said that we should come in on Saturday to discuss which way we would go. He spoke of a mastectomy or the possibility of a lumpectomy in which only the cancerous area is removed as well as the auxiliary lymph nodes. This would then be followed by radiation treatments.

It was difficult for me to pray, and I desperately wanted Troy and Cheryl, our dear evangelist friends, to pray with me. I did not have their new phone number so I called the state office of our denomination. Norma Rayburn, who had previously had breast cancer, answered the phone. "Peggy, what is the matter?" she asked. "You sound upset." I wept, "Norma, the doctor just told me I have breast cancer." She said, "I would go to Ann Arbor if I had it to do again."

Ann Arbor? My friend Barbara Yoder who had taught female care to medical doctors at the University of Michigan Medical School was now pastoring in that city. I called Barbara and told her my situation. She suggested, "Come over tonight and let me examine it. I still have association with the doctors I previously worked with. They can help us get you in to see a good breast surgeon." That night my husband took me to the Yoder's home. Barbara examined the lump which was as large as a hen egg. Immediately she got me an appointment with Doctor Courtland Schmidt in Ann Arbor. Barbara later shared her feelings in a meeting concerning my condition at the time:

> I have had years and years of experience in the medical profession and had examined thousands of women's breasts, but I had only found one tumor in all my life that was bigger than the one Peggy had. I expected the report to come back

positive even though I did not tell her at that time. But the truth of the matter was that God had begun to speak to Peggy through his prophets last April. My comfort was that if God told her what His will was for her, He has no intention of her dying. So we stood on that. God already knew and was saying, 'Fight a good warfare with the prophecies that have gone before you,' like Paul said to Timothy. When I examined that tumor I knew it would be a miracle of God if cancer was not already in the lymph nodes. I knew there had to be if things happen as they usually happen. There was no cancer in her lymph nodes. That was a miracle of God. God sealed that tumor off because the devil was trying to destroy her, but God had a plan and a purpose for her life.

Even though my friend was hurting with me, Barbara felt that she had the Word of the Lord that I was healed. But she was hesitant to be dogmatic about it since I was her friend. She went with my husband and me to talk with the doctor in Ann Arbor. When she was with me going through so many tests and knowing that this well-known breast specialist thought it was cancer, she said, "Peggy, just walk it through." It was comforting to have one with so much medical knowledge as well as spiritual knowledge walking by my side as I went from office to office for blood work, ultrasounds, reports on the size of the lump, etc.

My surgeon explained to me that the recent research by the American Cancer Institute indicated that the results of the lumpectomy procedure are as promising for survival as mastectomy. Breast cancer can't be prevented, but early detection is crucial. However, it looked as though this lump was not detected early. It appeared to have been there at least a year and maybe longer. I had been careful to have mammograms yearly. For some reason the enemy had kept this hidden. The mammogram a year earlier had shown nothing.

The fear was overwhelming. Cancer has three spirits: infirmity, fear, and bondage. This battle was the biggest spiritual battle I had ever fought. Here I was teaching that healing is in the atonement and this happens. I would be sitting with my family for a meal and fear would overwhelm me. The only panacea I had was to run to the Word. Anytime conversation would turn to the ordinary, I had to excuse myself and get alone with the Word of God. Then healing Scriptures leaped into my heart.

My daughter had a friend who was visiting us when this whole ordeal began. The day she had to return to Tennessee, we wanted to take her as a family into Canada. Before we left, I wrote out healing Scriptures and pinned them on my dress. We took Christie for a walk along the river separating the United States and Canada, and while my husband was entertaining the girls, I walked a distance away from them to pray. To the girls it was funny to see those Scriptures pinned on my dress. But it was meaningful to me. My daughter Sherri still has the Scriptures in her memory book as a memorial of that time.

In the midst of my spiritual struggle, there were all the visits to the doctor's office that had to be made. Early one morning I received a call from the hospital receptionist saying I had to come to the hospital in about two hours to discuss the radiation treatments I was to have after surgery with the head of the radiation department. This was all so frightening. The thought of my driving up to the Rose Cancer Center was overwhelming. It was a fight realizing that Peggy Scarborough, who believed and taught divine healing, was actually going into a cancer center. "A cancer center? What kind of victory is the devil winning?" I asked.

The radiologist was wonderful and reassuring. "Maybe your prayers are working and you won't have to see me," she said. June and Zack, dear friends who went with me to the cancer center, were in the hall claiming the Word for me. June almost shouted when she found Matthew 15:13, which became my "rhema" throughout the rest of the ordeal: "Every plant which My heavenly father hath not planted shall be rooted up."

Marion Spellman and her husband Harold, founder and directors of a busy drug-rehabilitation ministry called Peniel, cancelled all their appointments to come so they could be there with me and personally pray with me before the surgery. Nineteen other intercessors met me at the hospital in Ann Arbor at 6:00 a.m. on July 16.

Some of these intercessors had driven more than fifty miles and had left very early so they could arrive at the hospital before I did that morning. My family and I, along with the Spellmans, had spent the night in Ann Arbor, so my very close friend Sharon Strong arranged for them all to be there before I arrived. What a comfort to have nineteen people meet me at 6:00 a.m., not just to show concern, but to intercede until I was safe.

My friend Marion helped me write the Scripture references that had become "rhema" to me on the palm of my hand before going into surgery. The anesthesiologist asked me what those Scriptures said. I quoted Matthew 15:13: "Every plant which My heavenly father hath not planted shall be rooted up." To my amazement, he pulled out a New Testament which he was carrying in his pocket. What a blessing just before going into surgery.

When the doctor sent word back to my husband that the lump was malignant, the intercessors prayed the harder. While they were praying in the hospital chapel, the Word of the Lord came to June Pokley, saying, "I have not taken My presence from this situation; I will never leave nor forsake Peggy. Remain steadfast in the faith and behold the name of the Lord."

The doctor had assured me that he would not take the breast, but only the lump and surrounding tissue. Of course the lymph glands had to come out. Upon awakening, I was extremely thankful that the breast did not have to be removed.

Fear like I had never known before overtook me at times. I played Norvel Hayes' tapes titled "How to Live and Not Die" around the clock. When the tape would be over, I would awaken intuitively and start it over again. This saved my emotions. The powerful teaching of the Word of God pushed back the satanic terrors by night.

After surgery my emotions were very sensitive. Even the lady who dropped ice cubes in my cup made an indelible impression on me. The spirit of every person who walked into my room affected me greatly. Everyone walks in his own spiritual atmosphere and affects other people—especially those fighting such battles.

Cancer also affects family members. My daughter, who was getting ready to go back to college for her junior year, went home immediately after my surgery to battle through her emotions. She had always been my best friend. What now for her? Writing about it helped her. She grabbed a large sheet of paper and made a large sign that went across one entire wall: "God has it all under control." What a comfort those words became to me as well as to her. As long as we lived in that home, that sign remained on her bedroom wall.

The morning I was discharged from the hospital, I shared my feelings and fears with my friends, Herman and Doreen Smith. They lovingly advised, "Peg, keep on teaching healing." Then the doctor came in and said, "I can't give you any hope until we get the reports back. Your lymph glands looked clear to me, but I miss it as many times as I get it accurately." He continued, "The thing I am concerned about with you is the large size of the lump. The one thing we know about cancer is that it spreads and your tumor was very large." That report was most depressing. Then the trip from Ann Arbor to my home was a long and hard one with my emotions so confused. I could not even share my deepest feelings with my husband. There were insurance problems. What if the present insurance company dropped our group in Michigan? Would we ever be able to live in any state other than Michigan because of my now "pre-existing condition." All of this added more fear.

Arriving home, my only comfort was my tapes. I found it difficult to pray so I just lived with the Word on tape. I read healing Scriptures. I quoted them to myself, to God, to the devil, and to friends.

Three days later I returned to the doctor's office. Good news! The cancer had not spread to the lymph glands even though the lump was considered a stage two cancer due to its huge size. It was as though God had sealed off the tumor.

The biggest battle I had at this time was fighting off the evil reports that were constantly reaching me. One woman told a friend of mine, "With a lump that size, she may live two years." But then God would send the Word of the Lord to me. Carol Catalano, now living in Tulsa, called me. She remembered that approximately a year previously my husband had preached the funeral of her sister who had died from breast cancer. And of all things, her name was also Peggy. Carol said, "Peggy, what happened to my sister has nothing to do with you or the Word of God. Stand on the Word."

I refused to go to bed. I felt that to do so would be a victory for the enemy. Less than two weeks after surgery I was back teaching my healing class in the church on Thursdays. It was great strength to me to be able to proclaim to the people not to look at their symptoms, but to look at God.

Then I had to start radiation treatments, which is standard procedure for anyone who has had a lumpectomy. Even though I had read all the literature and knew what to expect, I was frightened that first day. My body actually trembled when the doctor and her assistants diagrammed me for the region that would be treated. They marked the radiation path with purple pencils that could wash off. I was told not to bathe the breast area until after the treatments were under way and they could tattoo the area. The big machines were terrifying.

The daily battle began when the radiation treatments actually began. It was a depressing thing to walk down a long cold undecorated hall to get to the treatment room. Then I had to put on an ugly grey gown to get ready for the treatment. I still remember feeling like a leper. Once in the waiting room, I would notice all the extremely sick people. The enemy whispered, "See, that is what is going to happen to you. It's just a matter of time." Once again I learned that I dare not go into that waiting room without the Word of God. While I waited, I began bathing my mind with what God had said about sickness and healing. The thing that kept me going through the treatments was the same thing that kept me going through the surgery—not letting the Word depart from my eyes or ears.

During the time I was receiving these radiation treatments, I found a package of literature in the mail that had been sent to my family. I opened it quickly, hoping for a word from the Lord. There were several small booklets. I turned to the first page of one. It was an article on how a family should react when the mother of the family gets breast cancer and dies. Another booklet was on the family's reaction to the mother's death. But the negative mail was not all I received. I received encouraging letters from people I did not know with prophetic words that I was healed.

Through many other similar incidents, I realized that God was fighting my battle. My daughter was back in college, and during the radiation treatments she sent me a plant with a large note, saying, "God has it all under control." These became our fighting words.

The numerous prophetic encounters discussed earlier were such a wonderful blessing, especially in fighting off my fear of the cancer reappearing. I waged war with the prophetic words. I reminded God of what the prophets had said again and again. Also the words of Nahum 1:9, "This affliction shall not rise up the second time," became a source of tremendous strength to me.

At the time of this writing, three and a half years away from the cancer, I do many of the same things I did while warring for my healing. My compassion for those with cancer is greater than it has ever been. During the time of crisis, I made a decision that cancer would have a new enemy. I asked God to let me be a cancer specialist in the spiritual sense. I developed an especially strong desire to help those whom the doctors say are incurable.

Family Miracles

Before David slew Goliath, he had already killed a bear and a lion. Perhaps one of the reasons he was able to deal with Goliath was because he had already seen what God could do through him and for him when he was keeping his father's sheep. I had seen God miraculously come on the scene before for both me and for my family. It was easier to trust God for the big miracle because He had already proven Himself to be the Healer in our home.

Miracle of Childbirth

When I was pregnant with our daughter, Sherri, I was an extremely busy teacher at Lee College. Never had I felt better. I taught English and Speech right up until three days before she was born. I had given final examinations, graded all papers, and turned in the grades for all the students.

Sherri was born on a Monday. But on the Sunday afternoon before, my husband and I had decided to relax and do some reading in our front yard. Forgetting that I was nine months pregnant, I sat down too quickly on the lawn recliner.

The following morning I woke up to find that my water had broken. I called the doctor, who told me to come in at 10:00 a.m. to see him. When I arrived, I expected to be told to return in a few weeks. However, when the doctor checked me, he said, "We are weeks away from labor." I said, "Does that mean that I go home and come back in a few weeks." He answered, "No, that means you have to go directly to the hospital. Do not go home for your personal things. Someone can bring them to you." He then handed me a slip of paper that read, "Admit immediately. X-ray. Hold two pints of blood." I had ruptured some membranes when I sat down on the lawn recliner and did not know it.

The nurse called for my husband to see the doctor. He said, "I know you have questions, but I do not have any answers. We are just going to have a baby today one way or the other."

When I arrived at the hospital, they began trying to force labor, but it would not begin. It was a terrible day. My blood pressure had become extremely high. Toxemia had set in. I became deathly sick.

That evening around 6:00 p.m., the nurses had checked me and found no sign of dilation. Then Pastor T.L. Lowery came into the hospital on his usual round of visitations. He walked into the room with my husband and prayed, "Oh, God, we need a miracle now."

Immediately the miracle came. Three doctors walked in at 6:05 p.m., five minutes after the nurse had said there was no sign of dilation. They came together because they had to make a decision what to do because of the seriousness of my condition. They asked my husband and Pastor Lowery to leave. They checked me and one of them said, "My word, the dilation is three-forths complete. Take her to the delivery room." We had our miracle. They then said to my husband, "Go for a long walk. If we are able to have a natural childbirth, it will not be until 1:00 a.m. at the earliest." By 8:00 p.m. our daughter had arrived safely. They immediately began testing her, expecting to find brain damage because of my toxemia. However, they found a perfect baby. The doctors later told me that whenever the mother is as serious as I was, they usually lost either the mother or the child. If the child lived, she was usually born brain damaged.

During that crisis time, I made a real commitment to God concerning our baby. Though we had already given her to the Lord, this was a special commitment—giving us both to the Lord. Often today my daughter testifies, "I did not have a choice but to serve God because of the serious commitment my mother made at this time when we both were hanging between life and death."

Husband Healed of Bells Palsy

Three months after our daughter was born, we moved to Fresno, California, where my husband and I both served on the staff of a West Coast Bible College. The move was a stressful one from Tennessee to California with a new-born baby. We were living in an apartment in the girls' dormitory because I was serving as dean of women and they needed me to be on campus at that particular time. Also, my husband was teaching five new classes with five different preparations and serving as outreach director for the school. Having such a busy schedule, he did not notice that he was having a health problem. One afternoon he came into our apartment and said, "My left eye is not blinking." We then remembered that he was not able to play his trumpet in a street meeting the previous Saturday evening for some strange reason. I insisted that he go to the emergency room at the hospital. When they checked him out, they diagnosed his case as Bells Palsy. They told him that it could leave his face paralyzed or drawn. But the students on that campus went to prayer and in eleven days the condition was completely gone. The healing was complete.

Chapter Seven

Reviewing the Battle Plan

We have reviewed the predicament of a sick person. Many people are devastated by the onslaught of sickness and disease. When serious illness does strike, often a person must deal with all of his unfulfilled plans, ministries, relationships, and financial problems. Life suddenly comes to a screeching halt.

The Enemy is Satan

The first thing that must be settled is who the enemy is. Tradition has taught us that it is God who wills that we be sick in order to teach us something. But satan is the author of sickness. Christ always uses the same harsh word, *epitimao*, to rebuke sickness (satan's work) as He uses to rebuke evil spirits. Furthermore, Acts 10:38 states that Jesus "went about doing good, and healing all that were oppressed of the devil." T.J. McCrossan tells us that the Greek word for oppressed is *katadunasteuomenous*, the present participle passive, accusative plural of *katadunasteuo*. This comes from *kata*, meaning down or under, and *dunasteuo*, meaning to hold power or lordship. The way this word is used in Acts 10:38 indicates that Jesus healed those who were under the domination or lordship of satan.[1] Every sickness, disease, and infirmity comes from satan.

Satan is the propagater of sickness. There are special evil spirits whose chief business is to make people sick. Luke 13:11 tells about a woman who had a spirit of infirmity eighteen years and was bowed together and could not lift herself up. McCrossan tells us that the word for infirmity is *astheneia*, the most common word in the Greek language for sickness."[2] There are also deaf and dumb spirits (see Mark 9:25). Satan has all kinds of evil spirits, and thousands of these belong to that group designated as the spirits of sickness. Likewise, along with many sicknesses come many other spirits. Cancer, for instance, has three spirits: infirmity, fear, and bondage. There is no wonder that Paul said in Ephesians 6:12: "For we wrestle not against flesh and blood, but against principalities, against powers, against the rulers of the darkness of this world, against spiritual wickedness in high places." The devil has declared war and sickness is one of his finest weapons.

We Must Know That it is God's Will to Heal

Before the solution can begin, the sick person must know that it is God's will to heal; otherwise there are no grounds for a battle with satan. Every Christian has a covenant with God that includes divine health. Yet the

Holy Spirit through the prophet Hosea said, "My people are destroyed for lack of knowledge (Hos. 4:6). Too often satan has won the war. Christians have allowed sickness to send them to an early grave. They have allowed sickness and disease to destroy their bodies, while the Bible is full of Scriptures telling us that we can be healed. They have been destroyed because of ignorance. Still, preachers are teaching that it may not be the will of God to heal everybody. Too many people think they are helping when they speak the faith-destroying words, "God, if it be your will, will you heal?" This does not help the sick person. It destroys him. God's Word is clear about His will. But it must get into the heart of the sick person as well as anyone who is warring for him or with him.

It is obvious from Scripture that healing and salvation go hand in hand. One of the many examples is in Matthew 9:22, where Jesus said to the woman with the issue of blood, "Daughter...thy faith hath made thee whole." McCrossan tells us, "This expression, 'thy faith hath made thee whole,' reads in the Greek '*Hé pistis sou sesóken se*,' and literally reads, 'The faith of thee has saved thee.' The verb *sesóken* is the perfect tense, 3rd person singular of *sózó*, I save."[3] McCrossan also examines Luke 7:50 where Christ said to the sinful woman who had anointed His feet with oil and wiped them with the hairs of her head, "Thy faith hath saved thee." McCrossan says us that "this reads in the Greek '*Hé pistis sou sesóken se*,' and literally reads, 'the faith of thee has saved thee.' These are the exact same words Christ spoke when He healed the woman with the issue of blood."[4] The same faith which saves the soul heals the body.

Warfare is the Answer

Since the devil has declared war on us and one of his finest weapons is sickness, the Church must learn to do battle with him. The truth of the matter is, one does not have to die prematurely. But he does have to learn to war. Spiritual warfare is never easy, but that is why it is called "warfare." We already have the power. Jesus has stripped satan of all his power. He has delegated His power to us, even before He went back to the Father to be seated at His right hand. He is still doing His work today through warring saints. God has a battle plan and the Holy Spirit will be the warrior's companion.

The Warrior's Life Style Becomes a Weapon

The life style of a warrior can become a powerful spiritual weapon. Therefore, the life style of some may have to change. Getting well must become a top priority. The will to live must be strong. The warrior must know his authority in Christ. He must gain deliverance from feelings of shame and condemnation and must know that God loves him and is not chastening him. He may have to continually remind himself that God does not have any favorites, but heals all who turn to Him. Seeing oneself well will bring a much speedier recovery. Goal-setting is essential. Staying away from negative people is a must. The warrior must speak only what God says, then stop. Fear has to be dealt with. Proper biblical nutrition will strengthen the warrior. Speaking in tongues will build up the faith of the sick person. The joy of the Lord will contribute to the healing process.

The warrior's life will never again be the same. That which the devil meant for destruction will become the thing that will make him a health specialist. If the devil sent cancer to one of God's choice servants, that warrior can become a cancer specialist in praying for and ministering to those who have cancer. If the devil sent a heart attack, that person can become a heart specialist for others with heart disease. If the devil sent sugar diabetes, the warrior can become a specialist in praying for people with sugar diabetes. The warrior who is willing to go through this training will be ready to take territory back from the devil.

Warring With the Powerful Warheads

The powerful warheads that will defeat the devil and sickness are the Word of God, the name of Jesus, and the blood of Jesus. With these weapons available, the Christian does not have to live in sickness.

God's Word dwelling in you is a powerful weapon in the world. His Word is supernatural and alive. The warrior must hear the Word and hear it again. He must read it and read it, over and over. He must meditate upon it. He must memorize it. Norvel Hayes says, "It does not take a lot of Scriptures to bring healing. It just takes one."[5] The warring person must find it and make it his. He must quote it. He must do spiritual warfare with it. He must not place it on a shelf and admire it. He must write it. He must act on it. He must give the Word first place in his life. The person desiring to be healed should plan his schedule around the Word instead of trying to make the Word fit into his schedule. He must make the Word of God the final authority in his life and believe its report, rather than the doctor's.

The name of Jesus is ours to use. His name carries authority in three worlds: heaven, earth, and hell. At His name demons have to bow. Sickness has to bow. Jesus stripped the devil of his power when He was raised from the dead. He then gave this power to His church to use on earth. It is up to us to enforce this authority in our lives with the name of Jesus.

The blood of Jesus is a powerful weapon for healing. The blood that flowed from the back of Jesus after the scourging has power to heal any sickness. This is why Peter, along with Isaiah, says that by His stripes we were healed. It is a weapon to be used to bring healing to God's children. Rod Parsley, who is an outstanding pastor, sums it up for us: "If through the filter of the old blood covenant the Lord was able to declare, 'I am the God that healeth thee,' then here on the backside of Calvary, through the immunized blood of His Son, how much better for us is God's healing Word?"[6] Because of the blood that dripped from the stripes and bruises of Jesus Christ, no disease is incurable.

Warring With Powerful Missiles
That Carry the Warheads

The warheads—the word of God, the name of Jesus, and the blood of Jesus—are powerful weapons to destroy disease and sickness. But they are carried by powerful missiles. Missiles in themselves would be ineffective without the warheads. But together, they destroy all strongholds.

The missile of praise and worship destroys demonic oppression and brings the Presence of God, which in turn brings healing. God inhabits the praises of His people. When a believer gets sick, the first and most important thing for him to do is worship God. Many people are healed simply through worshiping. Worship is ministering to God. Those who are sick should worship both alone and corporately. As a person worships alone, he can thank God that no disease can stay in his body. Corporate worship prepares the very atmosphere for the miraculous healing power of God. Praise stills the enemy. A person can praise God simply by saying hallelujah. He can praise with upraised hand. He can simply bless the Lord. He can make music with musical instruments. He can give the loud *shabach* shout. He can sing in the Spirit. He can praise God by thanking Him for things that are not yet happening. He should use the Word of God, the name of Jesus, and the blood of Jesus, in all his praise and worship. He should sing the Word, making up his own tunes to Scriptures. He should sing the name of Jesus, and sing about the blood. It really works!

A warrior can launch the powerful warheads through prayer. He can pray the Word; pray in the name of Jesus; pray by declaring the blood of Jesus; pray with authority. A person needing healing can pray and be healed in the same way in which he was saved. Furthermore, he can pray for others, expecting them to be healed. In places in Africa, many miracles are taking place through prayer. Benson Idahosa is one who regularly sees the miraculous take place when he prays. When the large crowds gather for his meetings, many come to be healed. Idahosa does not look for the people with minor cases of sickness. He goes after the cases that are humanly impossible. He ministers to those in wheelchairs, and those whom most evangelists are afraid to touch for fear of being embarrassed because they are not healed. He has even had the dead raised on several occasions.[7] Miracles can happen in our ministries when we pray, because God is still in the miraculous healing business.

The missile of confession builds up faith and brings healing. Faith-filled words put you over. Words can be a powerful force for the person desiring to get well. Jesus is the High Priest of our confession. He does what He hears us saying. The warrior must speak the Word of God, which will become a creative power that will work for him.

The missile of resistance is like dynamite. Resistance is something that the sick person will have to learn. He must treat disease like a devil and drive it from his body.

Norvel Hayes shocks people when he says, "I am going to teach you how to stop cancer." People respond, "You mean, how God stops cancer." He replies, "No, how you and I stop it in Jesus name."[8] Norvel teaches, "When a disease tries to rest in your body, resist the disease and say, 'No, disease, I take authority over you, in Jesus' name, come out of me!' " He continues, "Here's how I do it. I say, 'In Jesus' name, no you don't. I won't accept this pain. I bind you, Satan, in Jesus' name. Go from me.' Then I lay my hand on myself and continue, 'In Jesus' name, no. I won't accept this. I break your power, Satan, and I command you to take your hands off. My body belongs to God. In Jesus' name, pain stop. In Jesus' name, get out of me. I claim the healing power of God. No, you don't; not to me you don't. You can't, Satan. I know you want to, but you can't. When I say you can't, you can't.' "[9] When asked how long he does this, Norvel replies, "Until the affliction leaves." Once you start resisting, the pain may get worse. That's a sign that the devil is shaken and is trying to attack in a stronger manner. Continue the resisting. Norvel says, "If my pain is worse, I do the same thing I did the first day. Never change, never waver, never get nervous...Do this every day...Your confession must get stronger every day, not weaker...If the devil sees one speck of weakness coming on you, you've had it...He will dog your tracks right into the hospital. He'll dog your tracks into the grave if he can. The devil doesn't intend to stop or give up."[10]

The missile of binding and loosing is mighty. Binding puts chains on the enemy. It takes the key out of the door. The warring sick person should bind satan. Bind all of his angelic ranks. Bind his demon spirits of sickness. Bind them in Jesus' name. Then he should loose health. Loose the ministering angels. Loose the protecting angels. Loose the warring angels. Loose the Holy Spirit's power through yielding to Him.

The missile that breaks generational curses is seldom used; yet, too often the same ugly problems and diseases circulate through families from generation to generation. These curses can be broken. Marilyn Hickey declares in the March 1993 *Charisma* magazine: "To break the curses of past generations—their habits, sins and physical weaknesses—we have to bind the strong man who has carried that curse from generation to generation. By exercising the authority that Christ has given us, we take 'the house'—or in this case, generation—away from him."[11] If heart disease runs in one's family, he can break it over his life and for future generations. He does not have to accept the philosophy that just because his relatives died of a disease he has to be plagued by that same disease.

The testimony missile always wins! When a person shares his personal testimony of healing, others are blessed. While I was working on this book, I began to pray along with several others for a lady with cancer of the bladder. The doctors were preparing the lady for the worst. The day that Karen, the lady who supposedly had cancer, went in to get ready for surgery, she found a wonderful surprise. The tumors they thought were cancerous were no longer there. The testimony of this lady is already inspiring the faith of others. It is powerful!

Warring With the Prophetic Word

Another great missile with which we war is the prophetic word. The sick person can war with the word of a mature, seasoned prophet. However, prophecy is not the final deciding factor. The Word of God has already declared healing for God's children. Even if a person receives a negative prophecy, he can turn his face to the wall as Hezekiah did and receive his healing. The warrior must get the Word of God into his own spirit, then begin to hear what "Thus saith the Lord" for himself. Journaling is one of the ways in which this can be done. Once he gets his innerself quiet, he will be able to hear the voice of God speaking to him. He does not have to take the word of another.

There are many who have received prophetic words that they would be healed; yet they died. Prophecy alone will not bring the healing. The person must war with the other weapons. If a person does not take the Word of God for himself, he cannot expect the prophetic word to come to pass. But if one stands on the Word of God, he can then war also with his prophetic words.

The War is Fixed

Getting healed through warfare is worth the fight. The fight is fixed. God's Word has already declared our healing. For those in need of healing, I pray this book will be a valuable weapon in your hands.

Endnotes

1. McCrossan, p. 2.

2. Ibid., p. 3.

3. Ibid., p. 48.

4. Ibid.

5. Norvel Hayes, *How to Live and Not Die*, Tape 1.

6. Rod Parsley, *The Backside of Calvary* (Tulsa, OK: Harrison House, Inc., 1991), p. 94.

7. Interview with Corletta Harris Vaughan, January, 1990.

8. Norvel Hayes, *How to Live and Not Die*, Tape 1.

9. Ibid., Tape 2.

10. Ibid., Tape 1.

11. Marilyn Hickey, "Origins of Generational Curses," *Charisma*, March 1993, p. 12.

Bibliography

Bosworth, F.F. *Christ the Healer*. New York: Fleming Revell Co., 1877.

Boisseau, Joyce. *You Can Live in Divine Health*. Lancaster, PA: Starburst Publishers, 1983.

Bricklin, Mark. *Natural Remedies for What Ails You*. Emmaus, PA: Rodale Press, 1985.

Capps, Charles. *God's Creative Power for Healing*. Tulsa, OK: Harrison House, 1991.

Cerullo, Morris. *Proofproducers*. San Diego, CA: World Evangelism, 1979.

Cerullo, Morris. *Spiritual Warfare Manual*. San Diego, CA: World Evangelism, 1980.

Cho, Paul Yonggi. *The Fourth Dimension*. Plainville, NJ: Logos International, 1979.

Clark, Elsie. *Spiritual Warfare Manual*. St. Ann, MO: Elsie Clark Ministries, 1988.

Copeland, Germaine. *Prayers that Avail Much*. Tulsa, OK: Harrison House, 1980.

Cousins, Norman. Video tape.

Editors of Rodale Press. *Meals that Heal*. Emmaus, PA: Rodale Press, 1990.

Fair, Horace. *How to Overcome Fear*. Collierville, TN: Deeper Life Ministry, 1979.

French, Joel, and Jane. *War Beyond the Stars*. AR: New Leaf Press, 1979.

Gardner, Velmer. *Healing For You*. Springfield, MO: Gardner Ministries, 1952.

Gay, Robert. Sermon at two week Intensified Seminar, 1992.

Gersen, Dr. Max. *A Cancer Therapy*. Bonita, CA: Gersen Institute, 1958.

Gossett, Don. *Praise Avenue*. Pittsburgh, PA: Whitaker House, 1976.

Hagin, Kenneth. *How to Keep Your Healing*. Tulsa, OK: Hagin Ministries, 1987.

Hagin, Kenneth. *The Key to Scriptural Healing*. Tulsa, OK: Hagin Ministries, 1973.

Hagin, Kenneth. *The Name of Jesus*. Tulsa, OK: Rhema, 1979.

Hagin, Kenneth. "Faith," *Word Bible*. Tulsa, OK: Harrison House, 1991.

Hagin, Kenneth Jr. *Can I Be Healed* tape series, 1990.

Hagiwara, Yoshihide. *Green Barley Essence*. New Canaan, CT: Keats Publishing Inc., 1986.

Hamon, Bill, *Prophets and Personal Prophecy*. Shippensburg, PA: Destiny Image, 1987.

Hammond, Frank. *The Saints at War*. Plainview, TX: Children's Bread Ministry, 1986.

Harrell, David Edwin. *All Things Are Possible*. Bloomington, IN: Indiana University Press, 1975.

Hayes, Norvel. *How to Live and Not Die*. Tulsa, OK: Harrison House, 1990.

Hayes, Norvel. *How to Live and Not Die* tape series. Cleveland, TN: New Life Bible College, 1990.

Hayes, Pat. Tape of personal healing, n.d.

Hickey, Marilyn. *Be Healed*. Denver, CO: Marilyn Hickey Ministries, 1992.

Hickey, Marilyn. "Origins of Generational Curses," *Charisma*, March 1993, p. 12.

Hicks, Roy. *He Who Laughs...Lasts...and Lasts*. Tulsa, OK: Harrison House, 1977.

Hiebert, Albert. *Smith Wigglesworth*. Tulsa, OK: Harrison House, 1982.

Hinn, Benny. *Healing* 9-tape series. Orlando Christian Center, Orlando, FL.

Hunter, Charles and Frances. *His Power Through You.* Kingwood, TX: Hunter Books, 1986.

Hunter, Francis. *To Heal the Sick.* Kingwood, TX: Hunter Books, 1983.

Hunter, Charles and Frances. *How to Heal the Sick,* 6-tape series.

Kenyon, E.W. *Jesus the Healer.* Lynwood, WA: Kenyon Gospel Publishers, 1968.

Kenyon, E.W. and Don Gossett. *The Power of the Positive Confession.* Lynwood, WA: Kenyon Gospel Publishers, 1977.

Kenyon, E.W. *The Wonderful Name of Jesus.* Lynwood, WA: Kenyon Gospel Publishers, 1964.

Kordich, Jay. *The Juiceman's Power of Juicing.* New York: William Morris and Company, 1992.

Kuhlman, Kathryn. *God Can Do It Again.* New York, NY: Pyramid Library, 1969.

Lake, John G. *Sermons on Dominion Over Demons, Disease, and Death.* Dallas, TX: Christ for the Nations, 1940.

Law, Terry. *The Power of Praise and Worship.* Tulsa, OK: Victory House Publishers, 1985.

Law, Terry. *The Necessity of Faith,* tape of sermon, 1990.

Lindsay, Gordan. *Miracles in the Bible.* Dallas, TX: Christ for the Nations, 1977.

Lindsay, Gordan. *Why Christians Are Sick and How They May Get Well*. Dallas, TX: Voice of Healing, n.d.

MacCabe, Wade. *Wonder Foods and Juices that Flush Out Body Fat*. West Palm Beach, FL: Globe Communications Corp., 1983.

MacNutt, Francis. *Healing*. Notre Dame, IN: Ave Maria Press, 1974.

MacNutt, Francis. *The Power to Heal*. New York, NY: Bantam Books, 1980.

McCrossan, T.J. *Bodily Healing and the Atonement*. Tulsa, OK: Rhema, 1982.

Murray, Andrew, A.J. Gordon and A.B. Simpson. *Healing*. Camp Hill, PA: Christian Publications, 1992.

Norris, Jacqueline. *Healing Belongs to You* 4-tape series.

Osborn, T.L. *Healing the Sick*. Tulsa, OK: Harrison House, 1951.

Osteen, Dodie. *Healed of Cancer*. Tulsa, OK: Harrison House, 1990.

Osteen, John. Tape of Believers Convention in Los Angeles, CA, 1987.

Parsley, Rod. *The Backside of Calvary*. Tulsa, OK: Harrison House, 1991.

Pickett, Fuchsia. *God's Dream*. Shippensburg, PA: Destiny Image, 1991.

Price, Fred. *Is Healing for All?* Tulsa, OK: Harrison House, n.d.

Quillin, Patrick. *Healing Nutrients*. Chicago, IL: Contemporary Books, 1987.

Roberts, Oral. *Deliverance from Fear and From Sickness*. Tulsa, OK: Oral Roberts Association, 1954.

Roberts, Oral. *Faith Against Life's Storms*. Tulsa, OK: Oral Roberts Association, 1979.

Sanford, Agnes. *Healing Gifts of the Spirit*. New York, NY: Lippincott, 1966.

Sanford, Agnes. *Healing Light*. NJ: Logos, 1947.

Scarborough, Peggy. *J.H. Ingram, Missionary Dean*. Cleveland, TN: Pathway Press, 1966.

Scarborough, Peggy. *No Doubts Here*. Cleveland, TN: Pathway Press, 1967.

Sherrill, John. *They Speak With Other Tongues*. New York, NY: McGraw Hill, 1964.

Siegel, Dr. Bernie. *Peace, Love, and Healing*. New York, NY: Harper and Row, 1990.

Simontons, O. Carl and Stephanie. *Getting Well Again*. New York, NY: Bantam Books, 1980.

Trombley, Charles. *Praise Faith in Action*. Indianola, IA: Fountain Press, 1978.

U.S. Air Force. *Doctrines of War.*,Washington D.C.: U.S. Air Force, 1992.

U.S. Air Force. *Training Promotion Fitness Examination Study Guide*. Washington, D.C.: U.S. Air Force, 1992.

Virkler, Mark. *Communion with God*. New York, NY: Buffalo School of the Bible, 1983.

Virkler, Mark. *My Adventures with God*. New York, NY: Buffalo School of the Bible, 1987.

Virkler, Mark. "Prayer and Fasting Retreat," *Communion with God Newsletter*, September 1992, p. 16.

Wade, Carlson. *Bible Healing Foods*. New York, NY: Globe Communications, 1988.

Wagner, Peter. *How to Have A Healing Ministry in Any Church*. Ventura, CA: Regal Books, 1988.

Wagner, Peter. *Warfare*. California: Regal Books, 1992.

Walters, Leon. personal interview, March 5, 1993.

Wigglesworth, Smith. *Ever Increasing Faith*. Springfield, MA: Gospel Publishing House, 1924.

Whitaker, Julian. *Reversing Heart Disease*. New York, NY: Warner Books, 1985.

Wimber, John. *Healing Clinic Notes*. Pasadena, CA: Fuller Seminary, n.d.

Yeomans, Lillian. *Balm of Gilead*. Springfield, MA: Gospel Publishing House, 1936.

Yeomans, Lillian. *Health and Healing*. Springfield, MA: Gospel Publishing House, 1938.

Yoder, Barbara. personal interview, January 1990; July 1990; August 1990.

About the Author

Peggy Scarborough is a noted author and speaker. She has authored several books and has written for numerous magazines. She speaks at spiritual warfare conferences, healing schools, prayer clinics, and retreats, as well as on radio and television. Peggy has been heard on the radio in several large cities and in the Caribbean Islands. She is the wife of Dr. Neigel L. Scarborough. They have one daughter, Sherri.

Peggy taught English and Speech at Lee College for 11 years, and English and Bible at West Coast Bible College, where she also served as Dean of Women. She served with her husband in the pastoral ministry throughout the United States in California, Missouri, Tennessee, Oklahoma, Michigan, and New York. Because of her many contributions to the lives of people, Peggy was listed in *Outstanding Young Women of America*. She received her bachelor's degree from Bob

Jones University, her master's degree from the University of Tennessee, and her Doctor of Ministry degree from Christian International School of Theology.

After going through breast cancer in 1990, Peggy learned to war for healing. It was during this time that *Healing Through Spiritual Warfare* was birthed in her spirit. In 1993 she presented the manuscript as her dissertation for her Doctor of Ministry degree at Christian International School of Theology.

Peggy Scarborough welcomes the opportunity to minister in your church, conference, retreat, or women's group. She is in demand as a Speaker for spiritual warfare conferences, healing seminars, and prayer clinics. She and her husband, Neigel L. Scarborough, do revivals and Healing for the Nations seminars in which they minister together concerning healing for the nations, healing for the soul, healing for the body, healing for families, healing for finances, healing for the emotions, and healing for churches.

Neigel and Peggy Scarborough

Peggy would like to hear from you if you were helped or healed while reading this book. If you have had a healing experience that you would like to share, she would like to hear about it.

Also, for further information concerning health products, nutrition products, food supplements, or juicers, please contact the following address.

For further Information Contact:

Peggy Scarborough
110 Elaine Drive
Easley, SC 29642

I Would Like to Hear From You

I want to invite you to write to me. I would like to hear about your experiences. Also, I want to know if you are going through a crisis and are in need of a healing miracle. I will then know how to pray and help you to believe God for a miracle in your life. Simply fill in your Prayer Requests or Testimony of Healing, or write a personal letter, and address it to:

**Peggy Scarborough
110 Elaine Drive
Easley, SC 29642**

Prayer Requests

Dear Peggy,

Please pray for the following to receive a miracle of healing: _____

_____

_____

_____

Testimony of Healing

Dear Peggy,

Please feel free to tell of my healing experience from:

_____

_____

_____

_____

_____

Give a Copy of This Book to a Friend

Write to me today and request another copy of *Healing Through Spiritual Warfare* for you to give to a friend or loved one. Enclose a check for $11 and I will send it immediately so that you can be an instrument in bringing healing to someone else.

Also let me encourage you to plant a seed into this ministry, that the healing message might continue to be sent over the airways.

- -

☐ Yes, I want to plant a seed and be made a blessing to someone else by giving that person his/her copy of *Healing Through Spiritual Warfare*. Please rush me another copy so I can help a friend receive a healing miracle.

☐ Enclosed is a check for $11 for one copy of *Healing Through Spiritual Warfare*.

☐ Enclosed is a seed-faith gift of $ _____ for the healing ministry.

Please print:

Name _____

Address _____

City _____ State ____ Zip _____

Tear out this page and mail to:

Peggy Scarborough
110 Elaine Drive
Easley, SC 29642